HELLO? IS ANYONE THERE?

Hello? Is Anyone There?

A Pastoral Reflection on the Struggle with "Unanswered" Prayer

Roger Philip Abbott

Foreword by D. Eryl Davies

CASCADE *Books* • Eugene, Oregon

HELLO? IS ANYONE THERE?
A Pastoral Reflection on the Struggle with "Unanswered" Prayer

Copyright © 2014 Roger Philip Abbott. All rights reserved. Except for brief quotations in critical publications or reviews, no part of this book may be reproduced in any manner without prior written permission from the publisher. Write: Permissions, Wipf and Stock Publishers, 199 W. 8th Ave., Suite 3, Eugene, OR 97401.

Cascade Books
An Imprint of Wipf and Stock Publishers
199 W. 8th Ave., Suite 3
Eugene, OR 97401

www.wipfandstock.com

ISBN 13: 978-1-62564-014-7

Cataloguing-in-Publication data:

Abbott, Roger Philip.

    Hello? is anyone there? : a pastoral reflection on the struggle with "unanswered" prayer / Roger Philip Abbott.

    xviii + 122 pp. ; 23 cm. Includes bibliographical references and indexes.

    ISBN 13: 978-1-62564-014-7

    1. Prayer. 2. Apologetics. I. Title.

BV225 .A1 2014

Manufactured in the U.S.A.

Unless otherwise indicated, all Scripture quotations are from The Holy Bible, English Standard Version© (ESV©), copyright © 2001 by Crossway Bibles, a publishing ministry of Good News Publishers. Used by permission. All rights reserved.

Dedicated to all those who are fellow, impatient prayer strugglers in the Christian drama, with gratitude to the patient, gracious God who answers so much—and who, praise him, doesn't answer all

Contents

Foreword by D. Eryl Davies   ix
Introduction   xiii

1. Is There Really a Problem?   1
2. One Thing Is Clear   8
3. God, Father Christmas, and Prayer   21
4. Struggling with Prayer   25
5. Heartbreaking Prayer   40
6. Lament   45
7. Engaging with God   50
8. Trust Me!   54
9. Delays and Providence   57
10. Providence, Drama, and Mystery   63
11. Prayer to a Mysterious God   71
12. Omniscience and Omnipotence   75
13. Knowing the Answerer   82
14. Privileged for Accessible Grace   90
15. A Prayer that Cannot Go Unanswered!   101
16. The Final Answer—"Trust Me!"   106

Bibliography   113
Scripture Reference Index   115
Subject and Author Index   119

Foreword

I COUNT IT A PRIVILEGE to be invited to write this foreword. First, I have known the author for several years, from the period when he was a pastor and then later as he undertook doctoral research. During the period of his research stretching over four years, I was his primary supervisor so inevitably I came to know him well in the personal struggles and challenges of academic research. He did exceptionally well and I have been delighted at the way in which consequently a door opened for him to pursue post-doctoral research in Cambridge, where he is now Research Associate in Natural Disasters. We have continued to maintain contact and fellowship.

Another reason for my sense of privilege in writing this foreword is my respect for the author's integrity as a believer, especially in seeking to know and please the Lord whom he loves. In this context, he seeks to be governed in his thinking and behavior by the Word of God. For that reason he is prepared to challenge assumptions and statements that may not be biblical or that are not understood adequately within the flow and progress of biblical revelation. In this book he returns again and again to the Bible in an uncompromising commitment to establish what the Bible teaches on the subject. Context, careful exegesis, comparing Scripture with Scripture, and sensitive pastoral application to real problems are all aspects he takes seriously in exploring the Bible's teaching on the subject of unanswered prayer. That is why in this book you will be enlightened and challenged as the author takes you to relevant major biblical principles and narratives.

A third reason why I am privileged to write these words is that the author here endeavors to provide a practical theology for people as they face questions relating to unanswered prayer. He engages in biblical and pastoral theology that is intensely practical and contemporary. Consequently this is not a devotional book laced with exciting or sentimental stories. Illustrations are used sparingly and effectively but the rich biblical material that is handled contains a considerable amount of biblical narrative with which we can easily identify. Nor is this book intended as a systematic theology of prayer. Systematic theology has an extremely important place in the church, but too often it can be expressed or applied clinically and insensitively, and even become inadequate and unbalanced in biblical terms.

Practical and pastoral theology? Yes, the author writes from his thirty years of pastoral ministry as well as his specialized area of trauma response, in which he is now involved at an international level. Widespread personal experience also bears witness to the fact that many people, young and old, wrestle with this whole question of what is inaccurately referred to as "unanswered prayer." The author confirms this, writing, "Unanswered prayer represents a real and serious problem theologically at least, but also experientially, challenging bland and binary interpretations of Scripture."

But he expresses the problem more bluntly, too: "Why are there times . . . when God does not answer our prayers, given the weight of encouragement God's word gives us to pray—and how should we cope with this?"

He nevertheless acknowledges that some do not recognize the problem (chapter 1), while because of sin, there are some prayers that God will not answer (chapter 2). Here there is a searching, humbling, and thorough opening up of as many as nine or ten key biblical passages like Ps 66:18 and Jas 4:3, while chapter 3 offers further help for those struggling with the problem by explaining the term "unanswered prayer" as possibly "not the answer I wanted in prayer."

I found chapter 4 ("Struggling with Prayer") particularly encouraging, as it distills huge amounts of divine wisdom from key passages like Gen 32:22–32, 1 Chron 17:1–17, and 2 Cor 12:9. The headings are good too! The first one is "Let's Get Real!" Speaking of the Genesis narrative, the author explains, "Jacob desperately wanted God to sort out Esau. God was more concerned to sort out Jacob . . . Jacob needed to get serious with [the fact that] God has a different agenda." Another one is "Great Idea: Wrong Time, Wrong Person," based on David's genuine desire to build a temple for the Lord in 1 Chron 17. The answer to his prayer is "no" but "the Lord's ideas for us exceed those we have for ourselves." Is that not exciting and mind-boggling? "Heartbreaking Prayer" (chapter 5) and "Lament" (chapter 6) are valuable chapters, with the latter chapter explaining "lament" in many of the Psalms as "a frank expression of confusion and hurt to God."

Foreword

For me, the book climaxes in the final chapters. In chapter 9, in what are referred to as the "delays," providence always operates and the persuasive examples of Job and Habakkuk are used effectively to illustrate and apply the point of God's sovereign, wise, gracious, and universal control of all circumstances and events.

I am familiar with Kevin Vanhoozer's valuable book *The Drama of Doctrine*, so I was delighted to see that the author draws on this in chapter 10 as he places prayer rightly "within a dramatic relationship" and in what is an "unfolding drama, inclusive of mystery."

Chapter 11 highlights the vital point that "God has his secrets" (Deut 29:29) and "we must live with that," while in chapter 12 we are reassured that "God's omniscience and omnipotence provide him with ability to make such decisions, confusing to us but in a manner that is safe for us."

Have I said enough to persuade you that this is a pastoral and practical approach to the subject, one that is controlled and illustrated by Scripture?

A further reason why I deem it a privilege to write this foreword is that the book is about prayer. However, do not misunderstand me at this point. I confess that I am not a great lover of books on prayer. If I am honest, I consistently avoid such books! Why? Because they sometimes send me on a guilt trip or depress me or because they are so triumphalistic or simplistic and even possibly legalistic so that I cannot identify myself with them. There are only three or four books at the most that I value on the subject of prayer and that after many years of being a Christian, a pastor, and a seminary teacher. High on my list is John Calvin's glorious section on prayer in his *Institutes of the Christian Religion*. This is superb and I often return to those pages. They repay constant study, reflection, and prayer. The other two books are more recent but brief, honest, biblical, and encouraging contributions.

After reading and rereading this book by Roger Abbott, I have no hesitation at all in adding it to my small number of books on prayer that I deem useful and necessary companions. Here is a resource book I will want to return to often for my own benefit and for ministry purposes. No, I am not comparing Abbott with Calvin or anyone else. That would be a foolish thing to do. But the appeal of the book for me is enormous. For one thing, it is contemporary and tackles a pastoral problem that distresses and discourages some believers while disillusioning others. It is a timely book for that reason and one that scratches where it itches for many of us!

Foreword

A final appeal of the book for me is its honesty, frankness, and admission of confusion and of common struggles, while at the same time it provides a God-centered approach in which prayer to a sovereign, gracious God is so much more than asking for things that are important to me and my small circle. I am being called again by the Word through Abbott's book to engage with God seriously, to trust him, to cultivate my relationship with him, and to acknowledge that God has his secrets that I may never know. Such an appeal should be attractive for Christians in many countries and different situations, liberating us from a secular, worldly outlook that demands the "right" for us to know and plan our destiny as well as understand fully all that happens to us. The author sounds the important note that "trusting the Answerer *is* the answer for no answers!"

It is therefore a privilege to write this foreword and commend such a biblical and practical book to you for your prayerful reading, reflection, and response.

My firm conviction is that the contents of the book can be stimulating for preachers but also enrich the spiritual lives of believers of all ages. And I make no apology for insisting that churches need to use this book. For example, a corporate reading and discussion of the book's contents in family worship, church groups/Bible studies, and college/seminary meetings can only be rewarding and enlightening. You will find that this book challenges at its core the Western preoccupation with self, pleasure, and a superficial reading, even preaching, of the Bible in so many churches.

Dr. D. Eryl Davies,
Research Supervisor
Wales Evangelical School of Theology/University of Chester
Cardiff, June 2014

Introduction

PRAYER IS NOW INTRIGUINGLY CONTROVERSIAL. On the one hand, some secularists are determined to get it excluded from public life altogether: from school assemblies to the centuries-old rituals commencing local and national governmental gatherings. Yet, on the other hand, as the media reports on the casualties of disasters, wars, road traffic incidents, or homicides, we also hear the by now inevitable statement: "Our thoughts *and prayers* are with the family at this difficult time."

In other, non-specific cultural circles, prayer is much talked about and reflected upon—not just by Christians, not even just in the context of worship, whether liturgical or spontaneous. For instance, it is talked about a lot today in the context of the therapeutic: healthcare, counseling, and chaplaincy are examples of fields abounding in generic religious and spiritual vocabulary and practices concerning prayer, pertaining to different faiths and none. Of particular interest to me, as someone who specializes in offering pastoral care for cases of trauma, is the healthcare focus on prayer as a recognized, "scientifically proven" therapeutic resource.[1] We are assured that prayer is good news for the sick because it has been shown, in peer-reviewed research publications, to prevent, or aid recovery from, heart attacks and strokes; to reduce cholesterol, blood pressure, and cancers; and to alleviate depressive and anxiety disorders, among other health benefits. Prayer today is a recognized, valuable healthcare utility. In this sense it matters little who or what prayer is offered to by way of a deity, power, life-force, etc., or how it is made. It is prayer *per se* that is valuable to recovery from ill health on account of its meditative nature: that is, it is a form of

---

1. See, for instance, Benson, *Timeless Healing*; Pert, *Molecules of Emotion*; Servan-Schreiber, *The Instinct to Heal*.

Introduction

holistic therapy, which, in turn, is said to stimulate the healing chemistry within the human body. Contact with the divine or ultimate, however "god" is personally envisaged and perceived, is recognized as beneficial to health and survivability in critical situations.[2] Prayer in these contexts tends to be understood generically. There is resistance to defining what real prayer is: it is what it is in the eyes, and on the lips, of the pray-er.

I was discussing this with a client once and, in doing so, I made the perverse observation that in my experience I didn't find my acts of prayer particularly relaxing at all! In fact, I often found praying very hard work, as I wrestled with God over certain issues and then waited, sometimes anxiously, for his answer. Ironically, I had recently had a heart bypass graft as well—would that then amount to proof positive I had not been much good at prayer? Yet, I did recover well, so maybe I had become better at it? However, when Jesus prayed in the Garden of Gethsemane, or when Job or the psalmists prayed out of their distress, it didn't seem very relaxing either. Then, take those occasions, for a Christian at least, when one is praying in response to a deep conviction of sin that God has brought upon one, when one's conscience has been severely pricked over something (Luke 18:13). These can be times when a normally very laid-back sort of person can be transformed into someone in deep distress and painful anxiety. Those experiences also don't strike me as particularly relaxing! That offering of "prayer" (understood in a generic sense now) made by the prophets of Baal on Mt. Carmel (1 Kgs 18:26–29) clearly wasn't very relaxing (nor therapeutic given the final outcome!). But, most *un*-relaxing of all seem to be those times when I have prayed with great passion and urgency over a matter, and there has been no answer, no reply, just silence. I could reel off many things, and many people, I have prayed for in recent years—things and people I care for very deeply—and yet for these I am still waiting for an answer to my impassioned prayers. I can get quite restless about prayer, in fact.

Sometimes I am tempted to relax more, just forget I ever asked and put it behind me. On the other hand, I think to myself, "But you asked *God* for that! You believed something of his glory was invested in your prayer. You asked in good faith. So, how can you just forget you ever asked? In fact, how dare you forget you ever asked!" So, I wait on, trying to be patient; but

---

2. See the extensive work of Harold Koenig, for instance, in Koenig et al., *Handbook of Religion*. Koenig's research has been critiqued in Sloane, *Blind Faith,* and Shuman and Meador, *Heal Thyself.*

Introduction

it isn't always very relaxing. If I was someone who lived on feeling my pulse I would be sorely tempted to wonder if praying was more a threat to my health than an aid!

There is more to prayer than petition, of course. There is praise and adoration. Yet even in these, petition is never far away, for in worship we may passionately ask for the glory of God to be manifest in some particular way or context. I know Christians who have for many years prayed, in the context of worship, for revival, for God to restore the honor of his name in the church and in the nation. So perhaps I need to be clear: in this book about prayer, it is petitioned prayer, or supplication, for God to respond to an urgent need or crisis, that is chiefly in focus.

For Christian people in a crisis, supplication is often very important because it is how to invoke God's action in, and get to God's thinking about, a situation; how to understand God's purpose, assuming there is one; how to cope; and how to recover, all in ways that glorify him. Nearly everyone prays in some fashion if the crisis is bad enough, but Christians pray because they believe that in some way God knows all about their crisis, may even have caused it, can certainly influence it, and prayer is how they commune with God, how they lay bare their broken hearts to the God of all compassion. It is hard, therefore, when you come to God in this way and, to use the words of the late Oxford professor C. S. Lewis, you find "a door slammed in your face, and a sound of bolting on the inside. After that, silence."[3]

Lewis, writing of his experience of bereavement, spoke for many specifically in the dire throes of grieving for a beloved one lost to death; but his words echo the feeling of many who have prayed in earnest during any serious crisis in their lives.

Whatever the theology leads us to conclude, I want to respond to the way it feels. I am with the Christian writer Philip Yancey when he concedes, "Yet I know for many people unanswered prayer forms a barrier that blocks any desire to keep company with God. What kind of companion who has the power to save a life or heal a disease would sit on the sidelines despite urgent pleas for help?"[4] This book is an attempt to offer help to such people to keep company with God nonetheless.

Of books on prayer there is no end, from the terrific to the terrifying! "So, why another?" you ask. The answer is that for the serious Christian,

---

3. Lewis, *Grief Observed*, 7.
4. Yancey, *Prayer*, 208.

Introduction

little is so rewarding, and meaningful, and compelling as to continue in prayer, as when God answers prayer (Ps 116:1–2). Equally, little is so disheartening, if not despairing, than when God seems not to answer heartfelt prayer. The poignancy of this was brought home to me even as I wrote these early pages. I happened to lift from a bookshelf in my study a particular Bible to which I wanted to refer. As I opened it, a self-made note-pad fell out from between some pages. Being curious, I read the notes that had been penciled, as they clearly were not my own notes. It became obvious these notes were prayers which my eldest daughter had written some years earlier. She would have been then in her very early teenage years, I would guess. As I read them, I admit these prayers made me well up with both delight and sorrow. I was delighted to read the honest outpourings of my daughter's heart to her Lord and Savior, with whom she was sharing a personal sense of her own sin and weakness and need, and her delight in his grace. Her prayers effused praise and thanksgiving to God. I had no idea she had such relations with God, to such an intimate extent, at that age. To discover that was delightful for me. However, as a part of her prayers at the time, she would beg the Lord to have mercy upon her three siblings. She would plead with God for their salvation and peace. One of those siblings seems to have been a particular burden for her in prayer. This made me sad, for, as far as I know, that prayerful request has yet to be granted her, or me; for I too have been praying things similar to her, for much longer than her in fact, and answers are still being awaited.

Alongside of the problem of evil and suffering the problem of unanswered prayer is one of the most complex, yet common, pastoral issues I have found myself having to address through thirty years of church ministry. In the more specialized field of trauma response, where I now work, it continues to be a haunting, and daunting, issue to handle.

So, I thought to write this book because the matter of prayer going unanswered is a truly serious problem in all kinds of ways, both theological and pastoral. As you read you may well call to mind your own particular emotions and thoughts with your perception that God did not answer your prayers at times. In fact, I note that authors addressing the subject often like to pack their works with anecdotal evidence: usually touching stories from people who have felt let down by God because he did not respond to their urgent pleas for healing, guidance, relationships, exam passes, and a myriad other needs people treat as essential to their lives. Then there are those books on prayer where the authors feel they have discovered some secret to successful praying, and proceed to illustrate that fact by way of countless anecdotes where the secret has come good.

Readers will be forewarned I do not write in that vein; deliberately, I want to avoid spiritual voyeurism! Though I favor the value of personal narrative, I fear there is too much of this that is feeding the Christian book market nowadays. We all love a good story, usually with a happy ending; or, we can find some emotional "fix" through reading the heart-wrenching struggles of someone's story we just can't put down. This subject of unanswered prayer is, in my mind, too serious for providing brief emotional encounters, the reading of which seem to me to be not far removed from voyeuristic entertainment. Furthermore, no two stories are ever alike. Yet, like watching a good movie, we can become mesmerized by the hero or heroine and forget we still have to live in *our* world, when we put the book down.

The purpose of this work is to help strugglers with *their* struggle, not someone else's, so they can play their own part in the great drama of redemption. Yes, there are a few very brief anecdotes, to illustrate a point or two, but I hope there is more to think about than to feel titillated by. I make no apology for this. That is the challenge the Christian world needs to rise to if the world is to take us seriously at all, and if we are to take life seriously.

1

Is There Really a Problem?

I HAVE SAID THAT UNANSWERED prayer can be a problem. But is that strictly accurate? Is there really a problem?

Some, usually in the more conservative Christian communities, think that there is no such thing as unanswered prayer, and may see even raising the issue as somewhat mischievous. "The problem is not God's but ours!" they tell us with their Bibles wide open before them; we just don't know, through our ignorance, how to discern or interpret God's answer (which, clearly, they feel they do!). Indeed, Jesus spoke of people who, "seeing they do not see, and hearing they do not hear, nor do they understand" (Matt 13:13). That is, the answer is there, but some just never understand it. It would seem, therefore, that if there is a problem it must lie with us not hearing God's speech, with our ignorance or with our immature impatience. Therefore, we are perverse to even think of raising the matter.

When writing this book I took the opportunity of asking some friends the question, "Do you believe there is such a thing as unanswered prayer?" I recall one response was, "No." This person thought that all prayer is answered. He said, "If I asked you a question, you would at least answer it in your head, even though you might not verbalize it to me." I thought for a moment, then I responded, "But an answer in the head is no answer to me, in the sense in which we understand conversation to take place." In the discussion that followed we both agreed that it depends on how you define "answer."

Hello? Is Anyone There?

One can come at an understanding of "answer" solely from a theological perspective. The difficulty then is that we can try to play God, or we can try to defend God; either way, playing God or defending God is very dangerous when humans are attempting it! Defining an answer from God's perspective is not straightforward for us in strict theological terms. It would require delving into the eternal decrees, into divine omniscience and wisdom, even into the "secret things" that are not for us (Deut 29:29). Defending God over unanswered prayer is not necessary, since God can well defend himself. But, given the language Scripture (God) uses in revelation to us, I think "answer" can be defined pretty well. In Jesus' teaching on prayer to his disciples (Luke 11:9–13), he states, "And I tell you, ask, and it will be given to you . . . For everyone who asks receives." He then illustrates the point with the unthinkable possibility of a father, upon being asked by his son for a fish, giving the son a serpent instead. In other words, an answer is a normal, morally consistent response to a genuine question or request. So, praying that involves petition is about us asking a question, or asking for something, and an answer is God's direct response to that question or request in a form that is morally consistent with God's revealed nature. This pattern is what makes communication what it is. Therefore, silence, unless it is obviously telling—which it can be, as we shall see in due course—is not an answer.

Systematic theologian Wayne Grudem insists, "We must begin by recognizing that as long as God is God and we are his creatures, there must be some unanswered prayer." The reason for this, he says, is that God "keeps hidden his own wise plans for the future." Thus, the Jews prayed for centuries that the Messiah would soon come, and for centuries he didn't. In similar fashion Christian martyrs pray that Jesus will soon come again (Rev 6:10), yet despite the passing of centuries of suffering saints, Jesus hasn't. Yet, for so many of the cases of unanswered prayer Grudem refers to, they actually were answered, albeit following delays, or in ways unexpected. But, at least, as a systematic theologian, he is bold enough to insist that unanswered prayer must be a fact of life before God.[1] Since it is with the benefit of hindsight we can now judge that those scriptural examples of prayer were, in fact, answered, perhaps we should define what we mean by "unanswered" a little more narrowly. By "unanswered" prayer we mean prayer that does not receive an answer within the petitioner's expectations

---

1. Grudem, *Systematic Theology*, 391–92.

or comprehension, for this would be the criterion that a pray-er would judge an "answer" by.

As a practical theologian, my preference is to start where the problem is—in Christian and pastoral experience. At this level, which is the level pastoral care must certainly never shirk, I suggest unanswered prayer represents a real and serious problem—theologically at very least, but also experientially, challenging bland and binary interpretations of Scripture.

Where the problem lies is, perhaps, where many of us feel it most acutely, namely "on the ground." What happens on the ground doesn't always equate with the theology we are exhorted to be encouraged and inspired by in thin sermons or books. If that sounds to some ears like unbelief then I refuse to be repentant, though unbelief is the last thing I would wish to encourage! I do not equate my observation with unbelief or weak faith. I do not raise this issue out of a pique of angst, as if I am someone with a spiritual grudge or chip on his shoulder, aroused by a particular longing I have had in my life, which has in turn been expressed in prayer, yet never fulfilled. I am not one who regards God to be one's personal genie! Rather, I trust I can write with a pastoral heart, as one who wants to wrestle, both theologically and practically, with a phenomenon that is real and, at times, exceedingly distressing and confusing, in many a Christian's heart—unanswered prayer.

To put it bluntly: why are there times—at points, many times—when God does not answer our prayers, given the weight of encouragement God's word gives us to pray—and how should we cope with this? It is not wrong to ask these questions. Indeed, it would be a case of burying our heads in the sand if we did not ask them. These are serious questions to raise with a God who invites us to relate to him by faith, that is, by *trust*, and to take his word and promise as these stand—to even stake our lives now and ever after on what he has said. It is in endeavoring to exercise such trust that many Christians have asked God for things in prayer—not trivia now, not "Christmas lists," but serious things—for example, the pastor of a church in the Philippines I offered pastoral care to in 2011. There, more than thirty church members sought shelter in his church building, each one no doubt praying desperately for safekeeping as the flood waters rose rapidly; yet each one perished in that building where they sought shelter. I think too of those parents praying for the healing of some child who is suffering terribly; of prayers for the salvation of a family member you cannot imagine living without eternally; of prayers for wisdom to make a right decision in a heartbreaking choice; of prayers asking for some answers from the Lord when for months he has been silent at a time in your life when you have never prayed so much. The list of contexts is almost endless!

Now, I am sure that experiences similar to mine and those of my daughter, referred to in the Introduction, as well as those Filipinos in their flooding church, could be confirmed by countless other Christians all over the world: people who are trying to wrestle in prayer, but who are also wrestling over *unanswered prayer* in regard to matters that are breaking their hearts daily. Recently I was conducting interviews among Christians in Haiti, concerning their experience of a catastrophic earthquake back in January 2010. I heard tales of Christians who had gathered together in a church building for a prayer meeting—communing with God—when suddenly the building collapsed on them, killing them all.

Not least is unanswered prayer problematic because it seems to undermine one of the most profound truths at the very heart of Christian theology. That truth is that the Christian God is a God who hears prayer, and this is a significant aspect of his character, one that makes this God famously attractive (Ps 65:2) and worth knowing. In this respect, "hearing" is the same as "answering." God's fame is not that he benignly hears our cries, but that he answers them too. Scripture reinforces this in different ways.

Jesus, the Son of God—God in human flesh—drew upon the most powerfully illustrative forms of human relationship to stress this very principle (Luke 11:1-13). One of his disciples asked him to teach them how to pray. They had observed him in prayer and presumably had become challenged by what they had observed, and they asked Jesus for help, so they too could experience such quality prayer in their own lives. It is clear from the direction Jesus' teaching took on this point that he was concerned to assure the disciples that praying was good because God *hears* it, God *answers*. Thus, he appealed to the concept of *friendship* as the relational bond that will always guarantee God's ear for our prayers. Jesus told of the friendship between the two neighbors. The neighbors' friendship ensured the one neighbor got up at midnight to help out his fellow neighbor, who had awakened him for some bread for a late visitor. So, too, the friendship between God and the Christian should be the assurance for prayer. Because there is friendship, Christians can feel compelled to ask, seek, and knock, and on each account be assured there will be a successful hearing and answer. The friendship is the guarantee. Then, to ensure there can be no doubt on this, Jesus draws upon the most powerful form of human relational friendship—that between a parent and child: "What father among you, if his son asks for a fish, will instead of a fish give him a serpent, or if he asks for an egg, will give him a scorpion?" At the back of this, of course, is the idea that such parental deceit is nigh unthinkable in anything but very dysfunctional relations. So, it is even more poignant that Jesus could *compare*, not contrast, such a basic assumption between evil human beings and what Christians can assume to be true of God in relation to their prayers: "If you then, who are evil, know how to give good gifts to your children, how much more will the heavenly Father give the Holy Spirit to those who ask him!"[2]

Now, one accepts that, as in all relations, there are relevant contexts and conditions to be taken into account. However, generally speaking, the emphasis in these statements of Scripture is to assure Christians that God does hear and answer prayer.

This emphasis is only furthered by other statements from Jesus regarding prayer, albeit that these may well require even more careful reference to context. For example, "Therefore I tell you, whatever you ask in prayer, believe that you have received it, and it will be yours" (Mark 11:24); and, "Whatever you ask in my name, this will I do, that my Father may be glorified in the Son. If you ask anything in my name, I will do it" (John 14:13); and again, "Truly, truly, I say to you, whatever you ask of the father in my name, he will give it to you.... Ask, and you will receive, that your joy may be full" (John 16:23–24). Whatever contextual nuances need to be taken into account with interpreting these texts, they do serve to heighten the conviction that God hears prayer from his people. If these passages didn't have that effect then so many Christians would not have read them, become excited by their apparent meaning, and then become so confused when real life seemed to prove something different. Ironically, it is as Philip Yancey judges: "In a nutshell, the main difficulty with unanswered prayers is that Jesus seemed to promise there need not be any."[3]

The Apostle James seems to build on these assumptions. He assures Christians that when they lack wisdom they should "ask God, who gives generously to all without reproach" and be assured they will be given this wisdom (Jas 1:5). Similarly, Christians who are suffering are encouraged to pray, as are those who are sick. The latter are also to call for the church elders to come and pray over them, on the understanding that "the prayer of faith will save the one who is sick, and the Lord will raise him up." In

---

2. The parallel account in Matthew's Gospel says, "give good things . . ." (Matt 7:7–11).
3. Yancey, *Prayer*, 226.

this context of sickness, people are encouraged to confess their sins to one another and to pray for one another so that they may be healed. To inspire and encourage Christians to do this with confidence, James draws attention to the experience and faith of Elijah, the Old Testament prophet. Interestingly, the character of Elijah is referred to in terms that directly encourage us to pray. Elijah "was a man with a nature like ours." That is, we should not think of him as some exceptional character, someone who had something in his DNA that we don't have, which gave him some advantage over us in regard to prayer and being heard by God. The only extraordinary thing about Elijah's case was the God he prayed to, and that is the same for us. In terms of Elijah as a human being, there is absolutely no difference between him and any of us.

So there it is, a brief insight into the theology of prayer: the God-ness of prayer, which the Bible presents us with, to inspire Christians to pray. Fortified with such a theology, the Bible exhorts us "always to pray and not lose heart," when it comes to Christians experiencing contexts of injustice (Luke 18:1–8); to "be constant in prayer" (Rom 12:12); to be "praying at all times in the Spirit, with all prayer and supplication" (Eph 6:18); and to "pray without ceasing" (1 Thess 5:17).

No one can question, from such biblical material, the significant place and emphasis Christians should give to prayer in their lives, individually and corporately. Prayer should be, biblically speaking, at the heart of Christian culture and practice; it should be rooted in our mindset. For a Christian to find prayer an alien concept is like human beings finding air and breathing alien to them.

No one can dispute that there is a theology that encourages Christians to believe in prayer and to pray. Yet, in a book written in a very frank and popular style, titled *God on Mute*, Peter Greig affirms, "It is precisely because we believe so passionately in the power of prayer that we must also make sense of unanswered prayer. And when we do begin to wrestle openly with this issue, it can never be a neat, academic exercise for polite theological discourse because the question of unanswered prayer touches the deepest, most painful experiences of our lives."[4]

I hope this book may provide some answers to the vexing questions arising in Christian hearts when the heavens appear as brass, or when God has put us on hold or onto voicemail that doesn't get returned. I do not pretend to provide definitive answers, or an inexhaustible list—just some

---

4. Greig, *God on Mute*, 25.

pastoral care that might help. Mine is, therefore, a humble attempt to explore the issues involved in unanswered prayer, and to navigate pray-ers toward persevering in prayer with fervent hope, like the creation itself (Rom 8:19), which "waits with eager longing" for God to reveal his glorious ultimate purpose for his creation. The Greek word translated "eager longing" describes someone with head outstretched—as if standing on tiptoe in a crowd, trying to get sight of a special event or person. Too many of us make our prayer and then keep our heads down, forgetting that we even said such a thing, or for fear of what the answer may be, or from hard-bitten suspicion there will not be an answer, which is the harbinger of ceasing to pray at all. I will say some hard things, for that is how those who sense they are being cheated by unanswered prayer feel at the time; but do not be put off, I am not writing as a cynic. Follow the case as I try to echo the laments of myself and friends whose prayers have not been answered.

2

One Thing Is Clear

Given there is a problem in unanswered prayer, at least pastorally, it seems to me a ground-clearing exercise could help for a beginning. An instructive place to start would be to consider that the Bible does suggest there are some kinds of prayer God has given indication will not be answered; or, at least, we should never assume that such forms of prayer will be answered as we would wish. However, because God has stated so clearly these will not be answered, we can, at least, eliminate these from the problem! For example, God said to Judah, in the days of the prophet Isaiah, "When you spread your hands, I will hide my eyes from you; even though you make many prayers, I will not listen" (Isa 1:15). That seems pretty definite to my ears: God has said there are some attempts at prayer he will not answer.

Clarity about this is important, because we cannot hold God to a promise he has never made. Sometimes we may make a prayer regarding an object we are passionate to have granted us, and we find it hard to think, because we wish for it with such strength, that God could refuse it. However, before God we have no right to invest our personal passion so fully in something simply because we wish for it, when God has never given any indication of his perspective on the matter; we have even less right if God has said, "No!" Some people become so angry with God, even to the point of giving up the faith, because there was a time when they were absolutely desperate for something—some relationship to develop well, some healing for a loved one or for themselves, some success in an exam or in a promotion bid at work—and they feel God has let them down by not answering their prayers.

It is fundamental to the God-ness of God that he is not some kind of genie, here to provide our fondest wishes at will. To engage with the living God is serious. In many ways, true prayer is thinking God's thoughts after him, being in tune with the divine will and understanding just what God has said or promised, and, equally, what he has not said or promised. If we can never take "No" for an answer we will be in trouble in the Christian life, just as any child who cannot do the same will be at home.

So, in this chapter we shall consider some passages in the Bible where God has spoken about prayers he will not answer. Then, maybe, at least *some* of the problem of unanswered prayers can be resolved.

"So, don't even think of asking when . . ."

Sin Is Being Cherished

In Ps 66 the author writes a psalm of great praise to God for the fact that God has done awesome deeds and brought his people through huge tests. In a finale, where he celebrates God as a prayer-hearing God, the author makes this intriguing statement: "If I had cherished iniquity in my heart the Lord would not have listened" (v. 18). Now, there are two ways of taking this statement in context: either we believe the psalmist was using the fact that God had answered his prayer as proof of his not cherishing sin, or he was expressing a fundamental aspect of his concept of prayer in relation to the Lord: one must not cherish iniquity in one's heart, and if one is doing so, then one shouldn't ask for anything. My understanding lies with the latter view over against the former, more self-righteous approach. Either way it raises a real problem, doesn't it? Who of us can guarantee that we are free from sin whenever we pray? Sin remains part of the fabric of the redeemed sinner throughout this life (1 John 1:8, 10). So, the key aspect has to be "cherished": "If I had cherished iniquity in my heart." No Christian can profess to be free from all sin; but no Christian has to cherish sin in their heart. The two statements are not the same. One admits the lifelong process of sanctifying grace, whereby the Christian struggles through the tension between the desires of the flesh and the desires of the Spirit (Gal 5:17;

Hello? Is Anyone There?

1 John 1:6–10). Every Christian is a work in progress (Phil 1:6), and, therefore, experiences that relentless struggle; no one is exempt, no matter how progressed their holiness may be. But that is quite different from clutching onto sin and cherishing it in one's heart. What is the difference? John Calvin states it thus: "Besides, to regard iniquity in the heart, does not mean to be conscious of sin,—for all the Lord's people must see their sins and be grieved for them, and this is rather praiseworthy than condemnable;—but to be bent upon the practice of iniquity."[1] So, to "cherish" sin is to applaud it, to be in admiration of it, to be resolute in practicing it. The Greek Septuagint version of the Old Testament (LXX) actually uses the word εθεωρουν, meaning "to spectate" or "to gaze." I would suggest the term *ogle* is appropriate. If we can't take the eyes of our hearts off some sin, if it means that much to us, if the emotional tie is that strong, then we should not be asking God for anything except forgiveness, which would require repentance, which ogling over sin is not.

In fact, we have an occasion, recorded in 1 Sam 8:1–18, that is illustrative of this "cherishing" of sin, and where it is stated explicitly that God will not hear such prayer. This incident concerns the people of Israel demanding a king, to replace the more direct rule of the Lord through judges. The Lord instructs the judge and prophet Samuel to remind the people of how the Lord had taken care of them thus far and to warn them of how worse off their life would be under a king. Even worse, because they were effectively rejecting the Lord in making this demand, and because having the king meant so much more to them than having the Lord, it is stated categorically, "And in that day that you cry out because of your king, whom you have chosen for yourselves; but the LORD will not answer you in that day" (v. 18). God would not answer because the people would be crying out for help but not for conversion of their hearts.

Another reflection in Scripture confirms the unanswering of prayer while cherishing sin. There were few more difficult, confusing, and traumatic times recorded in the Bible than the times of the exile of Judah to Babylon, and few individuals for whom this anguish must have been more true than for the prophet Jeremiah. He must have seen, heard, and smelled terrible things: scenes of violence, slaughter, famine and desolation, all within a spiritual climate of religious hardness. As a man of prayer himself, sensitive to his isolation, these things were hard to bear and none more so than unanswered prayer. At one point, speaking for the whole of God's

---

1. Calvin, *Book of Psalms*, 478.

people in exile, he wrote of God: "you have wrapped yourself with a cloud so that no prayer can pass through. You have made us scum and garbage among the peoples" (Lam 3:44–45). Christians have sometimes reflected on their experience of praying and have commented, "The heavens seemed as brass." In other words, it seemed to them that God just doesn't answer; words of prayer just resound off some impenetrable cloud around the heavens. Well, for God's people in Jeremiah's day it seemed as if God had disappeared, hidden himself in a brass cloud; there was no way through, no connection. However, the context makes clear that the reason for this clouding of God lay in the people's appalling sin. That was so evident to any discerning conscience that it could be said, "Why should a living man complain, a man, about the punishment of his sins?" (Lam 3:39). There was such a hardness of heart within the people that the plea could be made, "Let us test and examine our ways, and return to the LORD! Let us lift up our hearts and hands to God in heaven: we have transgressed and rebelled, and you have not forgiven" (vv. 40–42). Thus, it was in this context—of the cherishing of sin—that God had wrapped himself with a cloud so that no prayer could pass through.

So, until the issue of our cherishing sin is resolved it is best not to seek for anything other than forgiveness. To pray for anything above this should be considered a waste of breath.

Now, it may happen, at times, that it appears God answers the prayers of those who, at the same time as praying, are cherishing sin in their hearts. However, appearances are not always as they seem, and the principle by which Christians should live is that we can never assume God will answer such prayers—we must assume he will not. God does answer the prayers of those who are in a mess; but this happens when such people acknowledge they are in a mess and want to get out of it, not stay in it (Exod 2:23–24; Ps 40:2).

But if this is the case, for those who are not having their prayers answered due to their cherishing sin, there is a ready and encouraging remedy. It is to repent of the sin and of that attitude and to seek forgiveness, because then we can be assured we come back into the experience of the psalmist—"But truly God has listened; he has attended to the voice of my prayer" (v. 19). So, it is good to keep short accounts of one's life as a foreground to acts of prayer—to take a review of one's attitude to the sin in one's life, and resolve any outstanding issues with God first.

However, this is just a part of the approach to understanding unanswered prayer. It would be unwise to consider it the key to understanding everything about the matter. In other words, if one is experiencing unanswered prayer then it is not necessary to assume, therefore, that this is obviously due to some cherishing of sin in one's life, as if the unanswered aspect of one's prayers is what exposes the cherishing of sin in one's heart! The key lesson has to be simply this: *if* we are cherishing sin in our hearts, then that is a sure place for us to begin to understand why our prayers may not be answered, and this one significant aspect we can fully resolve and eliminate without further ado, if we will. If we won't, then we have a fairly clear indication of why our prayers remain unanswered, and we cannot complain that God has let us down, since he has plainly said he will not answer prayer made with that attitude.

Piety Excludes Justice

God has clearly given notice that he will not hear the prayers of those who have no real, practical interest in social justice, but who can pile on the worship times. There are numerous Old Testament passages one could single out, but there are two exceedingly powerful ones in Isaiah. They are Isa 1:10–17 and Isa 58. These are stinging messages!

In Isa 1:10–17 the word of the Lord likens Judah to the infamous populations of Sodom and Gomorrah. On the one hand she could keep up such an outward show of the mechanisms of worship and approaching God—things like sacrifices and holy assemblies (vv. 10–13)—but, on the other hand, the Lord says he does not desire this kind of display at all (vv. 12–15). We see how it all comes to a climax when the show-praying is described ("When you spread out your hands . . .") and the devastatingly explicit response is assured: "I will hide my eyes from you; even though you make many prayers, I will not listen; your hands are full of blood."

Isaiah 58 opens with a description of Judah's dilemma: on the one hand she seeks the Lord daily, with an apparent delight in his ways (v. 2); she even seems surprised by the problem of unanswered prayer. This is expressed by the people's sensitivity to their regularly fasting, which was always associated with prayer as well, and the stark fact that their prayers were not being answered (v. 3).

Now, both accounts go on to explain the reason for the unanswered prayer, namely, that the people of God, or at least certain employer-class sectors, had no heart for practical social justice, but used their religious displays as masks for exploitation and oppression (58:3–4). The answer to the problem is plainly and powerfully stated in Isa 1:17: "Learn to do good; seek justice, correct oppression; bring justice to the fatherless, plead the widow's cause." In Isa 58 we read, "Is this not the fast that I choose: to loose the bonds of wickedness, to undo the straps of the yoke, to let the oppressed go free, and to break every yoke?" (v. 6); and if the people would engage seriously with the issues of social justice endemic within their society, "Then you shall call, and the LORD will answer; you shall cry, and he will say, 'Here I am'" (v. 9).

So, maybe we have become immersed in our church worship meetings, and the commercial industries feeding them the resources: singing our worship songs, listening to the sermons, attending the prayer meetings and praying like no tomorrow for souls to be saved and the church to grow—but little answering from the Lord seems to be going on when it is all taken into account. Why? Maybe there are also some serious issues of social justice staring us in the face—even within the church community there may be cases of exploitative employers, or of employees dishonoring the Lord in their work practices. The work environment can be really cruel and sometimes even Christian employers and employees can be part of the cruelty and injustice. Or, maybe even in the very neighborhood of our church there are families being overwhelmed with problems of financial debt and in the grip of exploitative loan sharks, or overrun by drug barons and pimps preying on hopeless young youths, male and female. Perhaps there are folk with no access to financial or legal advice, or who have no advocacy, or folk with learning difficulties who have no idea how to navigate the system for advice and assistance. Perhaps there are homeless folk, or elderly folk, vulnerable to thieves and gangs. Perhaps, even as we are singing and praying, they are crying and praying for want of help and justice, and we have no idea they are there—or, worse, we know they are there but we have no heart to help them get the justice they deserve. It is easier, more safe and comfortable to carry on singing. Just think: our neglect can be the reason our prayers, perhaps even theirs as well, are not being answered!

Now, on the radar of some churches (often of the liberal sort), social justice has figured very prominently but prayer has not; on the radar of other churches (often of the conservative sort), prayer has figured very prominently, but social justice only to the extent that the people have prayed that they will not be distracted from the essential work of worship and evangelism by social issues. Both radars are seriously askew, in fact. To attempt to practice social justice without prayer is nothing but arrogance in the extreme; to think of prayer and evangelism without practicing social justice is a moral and spiritual outrage. It is difficult to judge which is worse, given the habit of both constituencies for slagging one another off. Either way, God has said he will not answer prayer offered out of this neglect.

Prayer Substitutes for Obedience

During Israel's exodus from Egypt under the leadership of Moses, there came a point where they arrived at the Red Sea just at the time Pharaoh had his army in hot pursuit. The Israelites went into panic mode and began to complain to Moses, wishing they had stayed back in Egypt (Exod 14:10–12). Moses sought to allay their fears by assuring them that the Lord would fight for them. It seems he then brought the people's complaint to the Lord in his own prayers, because the Lord responded with these words: "Why do you [Moses] cry to me? Tell the people of Israel to go forward" (v. 15). The Lord was not going to answer any prayers while the people forestalled doing what they had already been told to do. Prayers of procrastination will not be answered. If God has clearly instructed us to do something, or not to do something, then it is pointless praying about it, unless it is to get his help in obeying.

We turn next to the New Testament, to Jesus' teaching on prayer in the Sermon on the Mount (Matt 5–7), and especially to the classic text on prayer, namely 6:5–15, where Jesus instructs his disciples how to pray; but in so doing he also hints at prayers God will not answer.

The Focus Is on Impression

Matthew chapter 6:5–7 begins Jesus' teaching on prayer in his Sermon on the Mount. In regard to certain practices of prayer Jesus clearly intimates that some prayers will not be answered. In these verses Jesus has in mind those who use prayer to make an impression upon God himself, and worse, to make an impression on spectators. Matthew 6:5 calls to mind the Pharisees and scribes, who prayed on street corners deliberately to be seen by others. Verse 7 has in mind the manner in which the Gentiles tended to pray: piling on the fervor with words and passion, this time to impress the pagan gods into hearing them. Clearly, on both accounts the implication is that such prayers will not be heard by God.

No one should doubt the relevance of Jesus' teaching for today. Since human beings are inveterate attention-seekers, this desire to create an impression is deeply rooted in us. It even comes out in our most important religious practices, albeit to varying degrees in comparison with the Pharisees' agenda! We shouldn't doubt the possibility of coming to a church prayer meeting and being tempted to be more concerned about what other people present may be thinking of our praying than what the Lord thinks. That is one reason many Christians find it so hard to pray openly in such a meeting until they get used to it. They are worried they will stumble over their words, or that they will sound silly, and so on. Sometimes we can come into the prayer meeting and hope that the rest of those present will notice we are there so regularly. Those who can pray out loud, confidently, can become the stalwarts that will always have something to say at the prayer meeting. Pastors? Well, they just have to get the hang of praying out loud, or lose face quickly, because they are paid to do it!

I think sometimes that church prayer meetings are incredibly unreal places, taking into account what prayer really is. People speak in ways and in tones in which they don't speak anywhere else. Not just their vocabulary is different (this is understandable, up to a point), but even their tone and modulation of voice are different. Then there can be the grunts and muttered words of assent from listeners: "Hmm!," "Amen," "Yes, Lord," and the repetitive "Jesus!" I do not mean to be contentious. I know sometimes these expressions can be spontaneous and real. However, I have been in too many meetings for prayer and witnessed (and contributed to) a style and pattern of words that is too uniform to be spontaneous or real. It has been learned and has become part of the "prayer meeting show" that we have fooled ourselves into thinking is compulsory for an effective prayer meeting.

Ironically, Jesus said that these "prayers" can be *very* effective, in fact. He said they are very effective at getting what the pray-er wants: namely, attention: "Truly, I say to you, they have received their reward" (v. 5). This has been the intention of the pray-er, and it has worked! This means that if such pray-ers can continue at ease, and feel encouraged after such "prayers," when there has been no answer from God, then it is profoundly tragic: God has said he will not answer such prayers, so any encouragement is just kidding ourselves.

Hello? Is Anyone There?

The Intention Is Avoidance

In Matt 6:14–15 Jesus speaks of forgiving and forgiveness. It is an issue not without considerable difficulty, it must be said. Some people take the view that Jesus is teaching that forgiveness from God is conditional upon our forgiving others first. Others say this cannot be the case in view of teaching elsewhere that places forgiveness by God solely at the door of God's free grace. I venture to suggest that there does not need to be such a binary perspective. There is an alternative view.

This view says that forgiveness by God is entirely of his free grace and is not conditional upon our meritorious work of forgiving others coming first. However, a clear indication of our appreciating and wanting the forgiving grace of God is the fact that we will be at least disposed to forgive those who have offended us. To put it another way, if we will not be disposed to forgive those who have offended us, then we cannot expect God to hear our prayer asking for his forgiveness, because we clearly do not want that forgiveness on his terms; we prefer being forgiven without having to forgive. God will not grant such a prayer. People who want God to forgive them will have seen quite a sight of the sin they want forgiveness for, and this sight will give a certain perspective on the sin they feel others have committed against them. That perspective will dispose them to forgiving more easily, or at least to so desire. If that perspective is not there, then it is an indication that the forgiveness they desire from God is not genuine. Being disposed to forgive others is the fruit of divine forgiveness, not the root. And if the root of a forgiven soul is present then the fruit of a forgiving soul is inevitable. So, we ought not to ask for forgiveness until we have a heart for forgiving; we may not be answered.

Perhaps the most penetrating exposition of this is found in Matt 18:21–35, in what is known as the parable of the Unforgiving Servant. Here Jesus depicts, dramatically, the difference in scale between the massive debt we owe to God and for which we desire forgiveness, and, by all degrees of comparison, the absurdly lesser debt we are asked to offer forgiveness for to others who offend us. The difference is deliberately incredible in order to teach us the nature of divine grace in creating human grace, and, by implication, the divine justice of a prayer left unanswered where there is no such human grace being offered.

Of course, it would be naive to imply that the issue of human forgiveness is a relatively easy one for us all. There are aspects of forgiveness that are highly contentious, complex, and intensely emotionally charged.

Perhaps no field highlights this so much as that of genocide and ethnic cleansing. The classic work of Croat theologian Miroslav Volf, *Exclusion and Embrace*, leaves us in no doubt as to the complexities involved, or the heart-wrenching dilemmas facing those Christians bereaved during the genocides in the Balkans, or Rwanda, or the casualties of the apartheid system in South Africa. Here in the UK there is the much nearer to home context of the past "troubles" of Northern Ireland.[2] However, Volf concludes that, even in the most severe cases of being sinned against, there should be at very least a *desire* to offer forgiveness and for being reconciled, though he recognizes the actuality of this may well never happen in this life. Praying for forgiveness from God does not make offering forgiveness easy; there can be torturous inner demons to do battle with, but having a desire to engage in such a battle, and a heart to find it in us to forgive, is a start; it is faith as a grain of mustard seed (Matt 17:20).

Another text giving indication of a reason for prayers not being answered through avoidance must be 1 Pet 3:7. It would be easy to overlook some words slipped in during the context of teaching on marriage. In particular the apostle is instructing husbands at this point, who should live with their wives in "an understanding way, showing honor to the woman as the weaker vessel." Leaving aside the contentious gender issues and how such words would be construed today, the point is that a married couple being together, in parity, heirs of the grace of life, should be an inspiration for a Christian husband to treat his wife accordingly. Where that doesn't happen then the prayers of that couple can be hindered—that is, they can go unanswered. Now, it is unclear if this means the prayers of both parties can be affected, or if it is the husband's prayers only that will be affected. It could mean either. The main point for us is this: if husbands abuse their wives by not attending to their physical and spiritual care, then this will hinder prayer. If, for the moment, we assume this applies jointly, to both husband and wife, then it is clear that while abuse within the marriage is taking place it is useless for the parties to engage in prayer, except to plead for help, to offer repentance and seek forgiveness. There can be no separate praying of the kind that just avoids the problem and seeks some sort of spiritual solace in an individual, personal relationship with God in prayer. Prayer doesn't work in that way.

It seems this advice was supplied by the apostle as a sufficient warning to spiritually minded couples about resolving problems in the

---

2. See Volf, *Exclusion and Embrace*, and Tutu, *No Future Without Forgiveness*.

marriage—just to think that their communion with God will be affected if they don't. Avoiding resolution, in preference for the continuation of abuse, goes much further than just affecting communication between the married parties; it affects communication with God. God has said it will result in unanswered prayer.

Of course, no man or woman can expect to know each other well enough prior to marriage to ensure that there will be no problems once they have married. There will be problems; that is why we have texts like this one, to help us when they come along. However, this text does imply how important it is for unmarried couples to be mindful of how complementary and compatible they are with each other in regard to praying together. The apostle's words only make sense in terms of effective pastoral care if a couple takes praying together seriously. Of all the many things to explore prior to marriage, praying together should be a significant one. Avoiding exploring that issue prior to marriage may lead to bigger problems during marriage.

It is interesting that the Letter of James, which scholars believe draws heavily on the Sermon on the Mount teaching of Jesus, addresses the matter of prayer. Again, two references indicate prayers God has said he will not answer.

Where the Mind Is Divided

In the first of these references, Jas 1:7, we are assured that a "doubled-minded man, unstable in all his ways," will not receive anything from the Lord. So, what is a "double-minded" person? The context is about handling oneself in times of trials and testing (vv. 2–3). We are told that handling these issues properly will be a constructive exercise resulting in increased steadfastness, or perseverance. But, handling trials is not a straightforward business; issues become fuzzy, and binary thinking can increase problems. The stress and pressure and pain can make decisive thinking difficult. So, the need for wisdom—to make the right decisions, to know what to say and do—becomes crucial. Hence, James encourages us to never hesitate in asking God for this wisdom, because God "gives generously to all without reproach" (v. 5). It remains, however, that there is one important caveat to that promise, namely, our desire for divine wisdom has to be real and not a matter of doubt. We cannot be of two minds about it; we cannot be ambivalent about what it might mean for us in the decisions we shall be led to make by this wisdom (which, in the context of first-century church life, could have meant losing your family, job, or life while under persecution).

God's wisdom, though it is the best wisdom, is not always best suited to our natural desires; it can mean self-denial when we prefer self-gratification. We have to choose which we want before we think of praying for wisdom. Hesitation would be tantamount to moral and spiritual instability. Prayer made while in such a state will not be answered.

In pastoral care I have encountered a number of people who have deliberately sought help and advice on an issue, but it has been a complete waste of my time and theirs, because it has become very clear that they only want to accept what they have already made up their own minds to do; they are not for changing course. So, I am left wondering, "Why did you even ask?!" We can imagine God feeling the same exasperation over some of our prayers. We can imagine him saying, "Don't come back until you are *really* ready to accept the wisdom I give."

We Don't Ask Properly

In Jas 4:3 we have a very explicit statement: "You ask and do not receive, because you ask wrongly, to spend it on your passions." This is a sequel statement to the fact that the people referred to often did not even ask God at all; instead, they would take matters into their own hands. It seems James had in mind here some Christians who were behaving, socially and economically, as arrogant, greedy materialists (v. 16), with a passion for making money at others' expense. This practical atheism draws some of the most severe warning found in the New Testament (vv. 1–17). It is interesting that in the light of the previous discussion, where double-mindedness was a cause of prayer not being answered, the worldly attitude in mind here amounts to the same thing (see v. 8). They would desire something so passionately that they would quarrel, fight, and even kill to get it; they would not ask, but would simply make a grab at getting it, by force if they could. Here were Christians torn apart by their own lust for material wealth, so that even if they did bring God into the equation it was to abuse the act of prayer by making their request out of selfish, materialistic lust (v. 3). It is impossible to think that the riches of gold and silver some of these possessed (5:1–3) were obtained in answer to prayer!

In a day when the Christian church, from a sociological perspective, can often be divided into the haves and have nots, enormous moral integrity is needed in prayer. Subconsciously, the lust for wealth can creep into our prayer life—but uselessly, because we ask wrongly. It is useless prayer because it is not prayer to the living God, but to an idol of our own construction that is made to appear as God. Or, to put it another way, we seek to use the living God as a servant to the object of our desire, an idol. Never, never will God become such in reality!

Conclusion

There is a strong case for concluding God has stated clearly that there are prayers he will not answer—prayers it is a waste of breath even to attempt. In summary, these are when sin is being cherished in our hearts; when piety becomes a mask for injustice; when prayer is substituting for obedience; when the focus is on impression not confession; when there is no heart for forgiving; whene there is relational avoidance; when the heart is divided in commitment; and when prayer is a device for our own desires. Being aware of these certainties should help clear up some of the confusion over unanswered prayer, even if it is only a preliminary ground-clearing exercise.

3

God, Father Christmas, and Prayer

SO FAR WE HAVE REFLECTED on the phenomenon of unanswered prayer and why it represents such a problem—or as I feel, in a constructive way, it *should* represent a problem—for the Christian. Then, by way of a ground-clearing exercise, we have considered Scriptures that make it explicit that there are some forms of, or attempts at, prayer that are a waste of breath—God has said that he will not answer them—so that ought to make that category non-problematic as far as our understanding of why God does not hear those prayers. However, life is never that easy to resolve by fallen human hearts and minds. So, perhaps some further clarification of just what is meant in this discussion would be helpful at this point.

Again, what, more precisely, do I mean by *unanswered* prayer? Is it not actually more accurate to say that all real prayers get answered, some with a "yes" and others with a "no"? This argument would say that the prayers referred to in the previous chapter are not real prayers at all. So, do I mean that getting a "no" as an answer is the same as unanswered prayer? Am I confusing the two? Ought I to change the subject to ungranted prayer or not-the-answer-I-wanted prayer? Why doesn't God give a "yes" answer to every prayer we make? But if this is what I mean, I would be guilty of assuming that praying is all about me asking and God duly answering. Of course, if that were true it would be the same as boiling prayer down to something like a Christmas wish list, and turning God into a Father Christmas figure. It would be betraying my own heart as that of a spoiled child, not as that of an object of divine grace seeking, ever thankfully and maturely, to grow closer in my relationship with the living, loving God, who has saved me from all I deserve from his holy wrath by choosing (in his grace) to love me more than I could ever imagine. So, let me be clear, this is not what I mean by unanswered prayer!

For the Christian, God is no Father Christmas figure—though, having said that, maybe the Father Christmas figure (as St. Nicholas) has its roots in the Christian concept of God being a "giver." Divine giving is at the heart of the gospel: "For God so loved the world, that he *gave* his only Son, that whoever believes in him should not perish but have eternal life" (John 3:16, emphasis mine). This is why the Apostle Paul could exclaim, "Thanks be to God for his inexpressible gift" (2 Cor 9:18). And James could affirm, "Every good gift and every perfect gift is from above, coming down from the Father of lights with whom there is no variation or shadow due to change" (Jas 1:17). Yet, extraordinarily, and contrary to the tradition of Father Christmas, certainly in the nineteenth-century sense, God does not go looking to see whether children have been good enough before he bestows his generosity. God hands out gifts to everyone, good and bad, and mostly to the bad (Matt 5:45; Rom 5:8, 10)! Yes, God is the supreme, liberal giver, because what he gives us are *gifts*, not deserts. Realizing this fact in itself can help us cope in the realm of unanswered prayer. The realization is that God does not owe us anything: he is not under obligation to anyone other than himself and to his word.

Even prayer is a gift. This is why discovering, and understanding, what God says about prayer and how it works is so important; otherwise, there is always the danger of our being held hostage to our own false assumptions, becoming frustrated in waiting for something to happen that God has never indicated will happen, even if we ask for it. For example, what if Moses had kept praying to be allowed to enter the promised land after God had told him he couldn't (Deut 1:37)? What if David had refused to accept that his baby son was dead and had kept on praying he would somehow be healed (2 Sam 12:16–23)? What if the mother of James and John had continued praying to God that her sons be allowed to sit, one at Jesus' left hand and one at his right, in his kingdom (Matt 20:21)? The fact is Jesus told her that granting her this request was not something he could do (v. 23). Therefore, the matter should have ended there, and probably did. There was her answer: "No." At the end of the day, answered prayer is a gift, not a desert, and some things we ask for just cannot be granted us, while others can. That is why we are instructed by the Apostle Paul to let our requests be made known to God in "prayer and supplication with *thanksgiving*" (Phil 4:6, emphasis mine). The gift of prayer is an essential aspect of knowing God, of our relationship; it is not about acquisition! In this relationship—where dependency is at the heart, where we abandon our self-will to the benevolent lordship of Christ—seeking God's direction and provision, and asking for these, is highly relevant, but so is trust. In this respect we ask in the hope, and dependence, that God will answer. But we must be able to hear and take the "no" as well as the "yes."

Nevertheless, assuming there will be a "no" to some of our prayers, there still remains the problem of *un*answered prayer. My own experience as a Christian and as a pastor leaves me in no doubt whatsoever that, in this respect, unanswered prayer is an experience, a phenomenon—call it a feeling, if you wish—that is common among Christians, even if it is not commonly aired as such. I refer, more precisely, to situations where Christians—out of genuine motives, and out of that developing relationship in knowing God, which his gracious act of regeneration has commenced in us—go to God in prayer and ask him to improve or modify circumstances. There then pass not just a few days, but weeks, months, even years, or at least what seems a disproportionate amount of time, and their prayer is not answered, either with a "yes" or a "no." Through this long period of uncertainty, there is no answer, only divine silence—silence from the God they love and seek to be faithful to as best they can. This is what I mean by unanswered prayer. Now, lack of understanding may well be a significant ingredient to this equation, I will grant; but, in plain and simple terms of how it feels at the time to a time-bound human, it is, to all intents and purposes, *un*answered prayer.

The effects of this experience can become profound if we are not careful. It can be such that the initial, excited faith, inspired by the kind of promises enunciated earlier in this book, which drew us into praying with such expectation of an answer, becomes dulled with disappointment and doubt over further praying. This, in turn, can create a dispiritedness and a sadness from the confusion and genuine lack of understanding concerning what God is doing—or, as it feels, what God is *not* doing. It can become most profound when prayer has been made in regard to something, or someone, that is exceedingly meaningful or precious, and prayer has been made with real urgency and sincere hope; or when what has been asked for most of all is wisdom, to know God's will for a situation, for some insight into a problem or choice that must be made—and it seems nothing is forthcoming in return, just silence. We all know how frustrating it can be when we urgently try to reach a friend by phone and all we can get is her voicemail. So, we leave a message, then another and another, but all we hear is, "I'm sorry I cannot answer your call at the moment; please leave a message after the beep." Alas, we don't even get a beep, let alone a voice message, when God doesn't answer our prayers—just silence. If silence could always be taken to mean "no," then it might be easier to cope with, but there are too many reasons, based on Christian experience, not to settle into the belief that silence must always mean "no." There are examples of Christians who have continued praying over long periods and have eventually gotten a definitive answer. There are those Scriptures that intimate the need for persistent praying. There is the conviction, even among a consensus of Christians, that the particular issue regarding an outcome or decision being prayed for is right and worthy. These reasons, and more, will not let us rest over the matter being left in unresolved silence; yet living and coping with that silence is hard to bear. Such sadness can feel like an unresolved bereavement, one in which there is no body to grieve over, and so no possibility of moving on; only now there is no answer to the prayer to come to terms with, and so no moving on. The whole thing reaches the crisis point when it strips the thread of our faith and we wonder if we have ever really been a Christian at all. That can sometimes seem the only conclusion to the binary between God's fame as the God who hears prayer and our own experience. Theologically, God's understanding, God's ways, cannot be wrong; that leaves us alone to bear the blame; there doesn't seem to be any other conclusion.

I want to help us see, like so much binary thinking among Christians, it is not that simple.

What follows is an attempt to help navigate such times, or seasons even, of unanswered prayer. I endeavor to achieve this first by reflecting on a number of Scripture passages where prayer is a struggle in some way—some from the Old Testament and others from the New Testament. In doing this I do not set out to resolve all there is to the issue, but merely to shed some light for the benefit of any who are struggling to cope with the God who, the psalmist tells us, is famous for hearing prayer, yet who sometimes seems not to hear yours and mine. In the rest of the book I reflect pastorally and theologically on relevant issues coming out of these passages before giving some focus to the immense privilege of prayer.

4

Struggling with Prayer

ONE REASON I AM DRAWN to the Bible is that this divinely inspired, written word is often more realistic about life than we are as Christians! A sensible reading of both the Old and the New Testament will show that prayer is not easy, not all the time, and that this is so for even the most mature and experienced of Christians. Men and women struggle with and in prayer. So, this seems to be an excellent source for reflecting on just what a struggle prayer can be for us today—legitimately so.

Let's Get Real!

Jacob: God as Adversary?

For my first reflection I have chosen the patriarch Jacob and his famous encounter with the Lord at Peniel (Gen 32:22–32). Now, this is not an instance of prayer going unanswered for long, it must be said—a mere twenty-four hours or so, in fact. However, it offers significant insight into the issue we are considering. In particular, it has significance for those situations where time seems severely limited, where panic has set in and we need wisdom and guidance for an impending crisis. Both of these factors were relevant to the situation facing Jacob at that time. Jacob was having a "chickens come home to roost" moment, a "payback" crisis from his twin brother, Esau. Neither of the men was angelic. Even before their birth they were at loggerheads in the womb (Gen 25:22–26), and relations went downhill from then on, not helped by the rather dysfunctional parenting that they experienced!

Jacob lived up to his name from the outset. His name meant "take by the heel" or "cheat," because, during the birth process, he had attempted to grab Esau's heel in a failed bid to be the firstborn. It seems cheating was in Jacob's DNA. He cheated Esau of his birthright, a most precious commodity for a firstborn male Israelite (Gen 25:29–34). This also led to his cheating Esau of his father's blessing, specially reserved for the firstborn son (Gen 27:1–40). It all resulted in Esau hating Jacob, and his resolve to kill Jacob once Isaac, their father, had died. Realizing Esau's intent and fearing for her precious son Jacob, whom she had spoiled terribly, Rebekah, the twins' mother, persuaded her husband to send Jacob away to live with her brother, Laban, in Haran. There Jacob served Laban for many years; and there he also experienced some "payback" as his uncle cheated him concerning Jacob's love for his cousin Rachel. However, Jacob then cheated Laban in return: through a rather strange sheep and goat breeding program, Jacob gained the flocks containing the strongest animals and cleared off with them, being instructed by God to return to his homeland. Though the rift between Jacob and Laban was healed, Esau remained a threat in Jacob's mind. He was tormented by the thought that Esau was out to kill him in revenge for his cheating. Therefore, when an occasion arose and Jacob heard Esau and his entourage of four hundred men were coming to meet him, Jacob hit panic mode. At first he hatched a damage limitation plan (Gen 32:7–8); next, he prayed (Gen 32:9–12); then he organized a number of "sweeteners" to try to appease Esau (Gen 32:13–18). Jacob was terrified, so he got himself alone with the Lord in a bid to secure the help and wisdom he needed to avert the impending, life-threatening meeting with Esau (Gen 32:9–12, 22–32). A prolonged wrestling then took place during which Jacob refused to submit to the Angel of the Lord until he had been blessed (Gen 32:22–26). So, this was a prayer meeting for Jacob like he never had imagined! It also suggests some helpful reflection on our problem of unanswered prayer.

What was the wrestling all about? What was going on when an angel, in the appearance of a man, confronted Jacob in a wrestling match? There is a commentary on this event given by the prophet Hosea (Hos 12:3–4), which throws some light on answering this question. The wrestling Jacob engaged in was in prayer—seeking God's favor. On the basis that the angel was no less than the Angel of the Lord, a pre-incarnate, theophanic appearance of the Son of God, in view of Jacob's claim to have seen God (Gen 32:30), then this means Jacob's act of praying found an initial *adversary*, not an advocate, in God! The wrestling, therefore, seems to have a spiritual and psychological (as well as physical) encounter, since Hosea says the wrestling involved weeping on Jacob's part (Hos 12:4).

So, here was a man who for many years had messed around with God; most of the time, he got through life by his own innate cunning and deceit. Now, when things have gotten really bad, he resorts to praying and pleading. In dread of the meeting with Esau, he really does want to pray as never before. But there is a problem: God is not so amicable, not so ready to get him out of a hole as before. God appears to Jacob as a wrestling adversary. Jacob finds his prayers are not being answered, not readily, and certainly not in the way he wanted. Why? What was going on? What is the explanation? Let me suggest some reflections.

Prayer Is a Huge Responsibility

Prayer can come too cheaply for some of us, as more of a routine device to get us out of a hole than a genuinely sought meeting with God. That seemed to be the issue behind James' rebuke to those practical atheists: "You ask and do not receive, because you ask wrongly, to spend it on your passions" (Jas 4:3). Jacob had prayed (Gen 32:9–12), but it may well have been out of fear of Esau rather than fear of God, because he immediately proceeded to do that which he had done for so much of his life—to hatch a scheme of his own making in the hope of placating Esau (vv. 13–21). That may seem a little harsh on Jacob, though, in view of the fact that he did appear very genuine in his design to meet with God in prayer after crossing the river Jabbok (the Hebrew word for "wrestle," *abaq*, is echoed in the name Jabbok). Even so, the reason that the Lord came to meet with Jacob more as adversary than as advocate may well have been to teach Jacob the huge responsibility of prayer as a meeting with God, not as a device for getting his own way.

My point is that delays of certain proportions seem to be frequently built into the exercise of prayer, to test the genuineness of our desire to meet God. Jesus, when teaching his disciples how to pray (Luke 11:1–4, followed by the parable in vv. 5–13), intimates this lesson. Since Jacob could have a tendency to take the quickest and easiest route, it would have been no surprise to read of him running away from this fight. Thank God, that didn't happen. It shouldn't happen with the Christian, either, when prayer seems to be a huge struggle with little happening. When God seems an adversary rather than an advocate, those who live by the easy route, who have no time to waste in a more prolonged battle in prayer, may conclude that God has let them down and they should give up. But that is because they have not grasped how huge a responsibility it is to meet with God; and meeting with God is not to be governed by our pressing diaries or calendars.[1]

Perhaps for God the most urgent need is not the thing we are praying for, but ourselves.

Jacob desperately wanted God to sort out Esau. God was more concerned to sort out Jacob. Esau was not actually the big issue for God, Jacob was, and Jacob needed to get serious with that fact. This is not meant to be a stinging lesson—one that is designed to hurt. I don't think it was meant to be so for Jacob, even though having his thigh put out of socket clearly wouldn't have been painless, to say the least!

I like the light Robert Candlish, the nineteenth-century Scottish theologian, throws on this incident. In summary, he makes the point that God's appearing to his people like an adversary also occurred with Hezekiah (Isa 38:12–14), Jeremiah (Lam 3:3–10), and Job (Job 10:6–20). With specific reference to the case of Job, Candlish makes these points: Job could have given up on God in cynical unbelief (Job 2:9); he could have taken the advice of his friends, that it was his own great sin that was the problem.[2] However, it was God's purpose simply to bring Job to humble submission in the light of God's glorious majesty and beauty.[3] Perhaps, sometimes, God's delays in answering our prayers have this principle behind them. We have some urgent, pressing agenda, but God has a different agenda, not unrelated or indifferent to ours, just more necessary and more wonderful: an agenda that will leave us in no uncertain terms aware of our total dependency upon God for how we go on in life.

---

1. This is not to imply God is never sympathetic to genuine crises, and pressures of time, in our world. He clearly is, as is evident from the way Nehemiah could present his "emergency" prayer when he was faced with the immediate requirement for wisdom during his approach to Artaxerxes, the king of Persia. Then he was asked by the king, "What are you requesting?" (Neh 2:4).

2. It must be noted that there is more than one way of interpreting the responses of both Job and his wife in this chapter.

3. Candlish, *Studies in Genesis*, 547–53.

Struggling with Prayer

Also, like Jacob, in the fight of prayer, we may well be left with some defect that we have to live with—some tangible, physical memento—so we never forget our blessed dependence upon the Lord. Perhaps some of those health issues that have hit us during the struggle with God, robbing us of the agility we had hitherto relished, and that we are finding so hard to bear, are actually tokens of God's strange grace in highlighting our daily need of him. In his *Call to Spiritual Reformation*, Professor Don Carson makes this comment on the Apostle Paul's prayer in Eph 3:14–21:

> He prays that Christians might have power to grasp the limitless dimensions of the love of God, so that they will be filled to the measure of all the fullness of God. . . . It takes nothing less than the power of God to enable us to grasp the love of Christ. Part of our deep "me-ism" is manifested in such independence that we do not really want to get so close to God that we feel dependent upon him, swamped by his love. . . . Paul prays for power so that we will be controlled by God himself. Our deep and pathetic self-centeredness is precisely why it takes the power of God to transform us, if we are to know the love of Christ that surpasses knowledge and grow to the maturity the Scriptures hold out before us.[4]

It seems strange to us, perhaps, that God should need to appear to a Christian more as an adversary, when he has assured us he is our advocate (1 John 2:1)—one who turns our prayer life into a fight not a tryst. But this is how it can be, and it is not for us to conclude that God is against us, to the point of hopeless despair, but rather that in his mysterious providence, which can appear with such a frown at times, God has something more wonderful to teach us. Meanwhile he puts what *we* want on hold. Prayer is this serious. It is not a gaming device!

By no means is this the universal answer to all unanswered prayer, but getting real in meeting with God may fit, and help in, the context of some who are perplexed.

David: Great Idea—Wrong Time, Wrong Person!

David, the Old Testmant hero king, who was a significant person in the human lineage of Jesus (Matt 1:6; Luke 2:4) and who became renowned for his psalmic prayers, had some experience of what might have seemed unanswered prayer. It occurred in regard to an intense ambition David had: to

---

4. Carson, *Call to Spiritual Reformation*, 196–97.

build the Lord God a house to dwell in, the temple. The matter is recorded in 1 Chron 17:1–17 (cf. 2 Sam 7:1–17). To be strictly accurate, again this is not an actual unanswered prayer. It was very definitely answered—just not in the way David had anticipated. So, why do I include it in this reflection on unanswered prayer? Because, in my experience, this kind of answered prayer can feel like it is unanswered. We have spoken earlier of the times when God may answer "no": that is his answer. But to someone who has thought extensively about the matter prayed for, sought guidance over it, gained confirmation from authoritative sources, and whose heart has been so much set upon it being answered positively, "no" can feel like no answer because it is so surprising, and also hard to accept. It can be easier to think, "Well, no answer at all is easier than accepting 'no' for an answer."

The matter was that David had reached a strategic position in the development of his kingdom under God. The ark of the covenant had been brought back to Jerusalem, Israel's appointed capital, and placed in the tabernacle, and the people enjoyed relative peace from internal strife as well as their past perpetual battles against surrounding tribes. David himself was living in his own palace of posh cedarwood (a premier building material at that time). It then came to him that while he lived in his house of cedarwood, the Lord himself was living in a mere tent (1 Chron 17:1), that being, essentially, the construction of the mobile tabernacle. This just did not seem fair or right to the king, so he had an "inspired" moment: he would like to build the Lord a house. But, although he was king, he didn't act as a king might by carrying out his big idea without consulting his advisors. He shared this idea with the prophet Nathan, a man of distinction in knowing and advising on God's will. Nathan's reaction was very positive in encouraging David to carry out his big idea. After all, the motive was so good, so honorable, and the time was so right; everything seemed in favor of it being God's idea too. However, that same night, God instructed Nathan to place a stopper on the idea—well, not so much the idea as the timing and David's execution of it. So, Nathan informed David that though the idea was good, it was not the right time nor was he the right person to take it forward. In fact, it would be one of his sons who would do it, after David had died (vv. 2–18)!

Now, we are not told why God did not approve of the idea's timing or of David's execution of it. Was David being somewhat high-minded and patronizing in assuming that because he lived in a posh house God should live in one too? There are aspects of God's reply to the idea that

Struggling with Prayer

could suggest this was the case (vv. 4–7), but we can't be sure. Whatever the reason was, this big idea, which seemed to be so right, so God-inspired, so justified, was denied to David. Furthermore, David's acceptance of the will of God over his own will has to be admired. He acknowledged the grace of God in all the development and success of his kingship and realm, and he deferred absolutely and submissively to the divine preference (vv. 16–27). There was no petulance, no resentment held against Nathan or God.

For others of us who have had to come to terms with the Lord's answering "no" to something we have felt so positively was God-honoring, the acceptance has been more of a struggle. Indeed, we often interpret that divine "no" as an unanswered prayer, perhaps subconsciously hoping God might change his mind and give us what we really want—a definite "yes"—later.

How, then, can this incident be helpful to any who find it hard to take "no" for an answer to their sincerely made prayer? Again, one can only bring the light that this revelatory incident shines. There are a number of points worth observing, which could prove valuable.

The overriding point seems to be this: *the Lord's ideas for us exceed those we have for ourselves*, even when our ideas appear so obviously God-honoring. For all the short-term disappointment David may have felt when he heard back from Nathan the prophet, there was enough to indicate to him that God's idea for his own glory would bring more delight to David, as well as to God, than David's idea (1 Chron 17:7–14). Of course, it is a noble thing to wish for the Lord's highest honor. Indeed, that is one aspect Jesus taught Christians should seek most by their praying: the hallowing of God's name (Matt 6:9). The awkward bit about this is how and when the hallowing (or glorifying) should be done. Certainly, we need to have in mind that our ideas for this may not necessarily be the same as God's. Good ideas to us may not be assumed to be God's ideas. Well-conceived plans, noble plans, prayerful plans, are not proof of their being God's plans. Sometimes, in pastoral work, people have come to me with holy enthusiasm over a big idea, one they are really fired up about. Sometimes they back up their belief that it must be of God with words of Scripture, prophecy, the positive opinions of others, and the like. The trouble is that we can't bear it if our big ideas don't happen. Our disappointment can even make us turn on our fellow Christians, especially our church leaders—we may accuse them of quenching the Spirit and failing to catch the will of the Lord. In fact, maybe the big idea has a lot going for it in God's eyes; it's just the timing and the outworking that has to wait. Let's not wreck up relationships, or whole churches for that matter, just because we struggle to take "no" for an answer from God. After all, what is really important here is what God's will is, not what is ours. And we should never fear that deferring to God's will means we shall miss out on blessing (cf. Matt 6:33). God may give us the gift of a big idea, but that does not give us the right to own the idea, as if it were ours. We are just a link in a chain in God's workforce! Can it not be enough for us that we have been allowed to come up with the idea, but someone else in the church, at a later date, must carry it out?

Neither can good motives be presumed to be God's direction. There can be little doubt about King David's motives for wanting to build God a house. Peter, Jesus' disciple, was at least understandably well-motivated when he suggested James, John, and he might build three tents on the Mount of Transfiguration (Mark 9:5), even though he was struggling to know what to say amid that awesome incident. Paul and Timothy had the best of motives when they desired to take the gospel to Asia along a certain route, but were denied (Acts 16:6–7). Yet, Peter, Paul, and Timothy had to take "no" for an answer from God. Not for one moment am I suggesting that coming to accept such an answer is easy and should not involve a struggle. Sometimes it is in the category of a lesson that must be "learned."

Another accompanying point is that *good counsel must not be assumed to be God's timing.* In regard to this big idea of David, he could have received counsel from no more godly a person than Nathan the prophet. Indeed, it is to David's credit that he even sought counsel from a third party in the first place. Not all do! Some operate independently, without consulting others, and then take it so badly when they don't get their own way. David was not operating as a loose cannon. He sought, and obtained, the enthusiastic approval of godly others. Yet, if ever there was a clear indication that no servant of the Lord is infallible in discerning the will of God, then it is this incident and Nathan the prophet's part in it.

Sometimes, if not often, our struggle is heightened by the fact that *we have such a limited understanding of what God's big idea is when measured by our own.* This account of King David's being told "no" must not be read without taking account of how sensitive and gracious the Lord's reply really was. There is no hint of God coming down hard on David. On the contrary, the Scripture reports God pre-empting any understandable disappointment David may have felt. God weaves into his reply that he has a better idea for David than David had for God! David's plan was quite a small one, and very localized—the building of a house for God, there in Jerusalem. But God's plan for David was to use him to build a spiritual house of an innumerable amount of believers from all over the world (1 Chron 17:10–15), and this plan would glorify God more than David's plan would have; David sees all this once it is explained, and he delights in it (v.v. 23–27).

The Lord has not called any of us to be our own empire builders. There are a lot of big ideas that go around the Christian scene that seem suspiciously like someone's empire-building. If that is our agenda after all, then we deserve silence or "No!" as an answer to our prayers. That was not King David's agenda, though, as is clear from his prayerful and worshipful response to the "no" he received from God. The point is, can we also be so worshipful and content with a loving—maybe even partial—"no" or "not yet"?

I hope no one thinks I am implying that understanding God's will is always simple. It is not. Nor does God always present us with such a clear explanation as he did for David. There are aspects of this incident that are hard to grasp. In fact, for us they only become as clear as they do because we have the advantage of a much bigger picture than David had at the time. We read of God's big idea working itself out, resulting in a temple built by David's son, Solomon; of the temple being always remembered as David's; of the central place that temple had until its eventual destruction as a judgment and the subsequent exile of Israel and Judah; and of the development of a spiritual people, leading to the coming of Christ, from the House of David, and the birth of the New Testament church as *the* temple (John 2:19; 1 Cor 3:16; 1 Pet 2:5). What a magnificent idea! However, for David it was all yet to happen, even his own idea. So, this was no simple matter for him, and it often isn't for us either. I can think of many good ideas that I (and others) have had over the years for building God's kingdom—ideas that, at the time, we felt were given by God, ideas that would advance God's glory and bind up broken hearts in his kingdom. Yet for some of these ideas we have had to take "no" for an answer, at least as far as our personal involvement in their fulfilment has been concerned. It has not been easy to do this, and perhaps the most difficult part has had to do with God and prayer being so essential to the thinking that had gone into the big idea in the first place. I guess the lesson from David's big idea is that our good ideas are not bad ideas necessarily; they are just not the only ideas, and they are not necessarily the best or the whole picture. Only God has the whole picture, and we should trust him in this when he happens to say "no" or "not yet" or even "not you." I know how this can seem even harder than an unanswered prayer, where the prospect of a "yes" can remain; but sometimes "no" is the answer and we have to accept it as a kind answer, the best answer.

Daniel: We Don't Know the Half

Prayer has often been referred to as a spiritual exercise, along with Bible study, meditation, and fasting. In the New Testament, prayer is considered an essential aspect of the spiritual realm—of communion with God and as a means of opposing demonic spirits (Eph 6:18). To Western, modernist minds this dimension may seem strange, something we give mental assent to, because it is an evident facet of the premodern biblical record, but not such an obvious one in our modern mindset. However, it is, categorically, a central feature of the biblical worldview, and unless it is central to the Christian's perspective today also, our grasp and appreciation of the Christian life, and of God's ways, will be stunted. After all, God is spirit (John 4:24); thus to enter into the realm of prayer properly must mean to enter a spiritual realm. But another facet of that realm is the created angelic spiritual beings, some of whom are now fallen and malevolent, intent upon damaging the Christian as best they can. It is difficult to overstate the reality this dimension has in the Bible and in the recommended mindset the Bible encourages Christians to possess. The Orthodox theologian David Bentley Hart states it thus:

> In the [New Testament], our condition as fallen creatures is explicitly portrayed as a subjugation to the subsidiary and often mutinous authority of angelic and demonic "powers," which are not able to defeat God's transcendent and providential governance of all things, but which certainly are able to act against him within the limits of cosmic time.[5]

The book of Job also makes this assumption; hence we are given insight into the spiritual dynamics that are played out over the first two chapters, regarding the satan challenging God over Job's faithfulness. Some scholars take the references to darkness within the book, symbolized by Behemoth and Leviathan (Job 40–41), to be symbolic of demonic spirits, implying a

---

5. Hart, *Doors of the Sea*, 65.

cosmic spiritual darkness operating throughout the interactions between the friends and Job.⁶

I mention this as preface to a particular passage in the book of Daniel, which speaks of the bearing demonic forces may have upon what might have seemed unanswered prayer at the time. The passage is Daniel 9–10. In chapter 9 Daniel had read in some historical writings that the prophet Jeremiah had prophesied the exile of the Jews would last for seventy years. Believing the time was right, Daniel prayed that the Lord would have regard to his promise and look in mercy on his people and forgive them for his name's sake. Daniel set himself to fast and mourn for three weeks, during which time there was no more divine response; nothing was happening—so it seemed. Then, on the twenty-fourth day, Daniel had a powerful vision, a revelation of the glory of the Son of Man (pre-incarnate Jesus), which overwhelmed him. This Son of Man then explained that God had heard Daniel's prayer from the very moment he had prayed it. Furthermore, he assured Daniel that he had now come in direct response to his prayer. But he also gave an explanation for the three weeks of silence and delay, namely, that he, the Son of Man, had been opposed by the prince of the kingdom of Persia for twenty-one days. Then Michael, one of the chief princes, had come to help him (see Dan 10:11–14). This imagery is somewhat similar to what we read in the Revelation (e.g., chapter 12), which only further serves to present the biblical cosmic worldview.

So, what should we understand about what is happening on the cosmic level and having a bearing upon the prayers of Christians? I would not presume to know all the answers to interpreting this passage in Daniel. However, what seems clear is that there is a lot happening on the cosmic level that is unseen to us at our terrestrial level. Not only do Christians have a battle on their hands, so does God! Evil spirits are able to exercise some kind of malign spiritual interference in the ways of God, for a time; this can cause delays in prayer that can make it seem as if prayers are unanswered. Anything more than this, I believe, is speculative. Some find in this passage a basis for their belief in so-called territorial spirits—that is, that there are demonic spirits specific to geographical territories (in this instance a spirit prince of Persia). The author Frank Peretti has done much to popularize this view in his very dramatic novels.⁷ Compelling reading though these books make, I have grave doubts about the underlying theology regard-

---

6. See Fyall, *Now My Eyes Have Seen You*, chs. 6 and 7.
7. For example, Peretti, *This Present Darkness*.

ing specifically territorial spirits. It is highly likely that the term "prince of Persia" is an umbrella term for all the demonic spirits doing their dirty business behind the scenes of Persian politics at that time. It is questionable to what extent taking on these forces in spiritual warfare by claiming back for God the specific geographical areas is commended, or if such is authorized by Scripture.

Speculation aside, what we do know from this account is that God does hear prayers during times when we do not think he does, but, owing to spiritual malevolence at the cosmic level, he cannot respond immediately; *he is delayed, but we are heard.*

This also indicates *what seriously hard work prayer can be*. However strong our views on the omnipotence of God are, they should not lead us to minimize the problems demonic beings can cause. Prayer can be presumed to be too easy for some. Just put in your request and God will answer it is the impression some Christians give; and if you don't get an answer immediately, it is due to your weak faith, or to some sin in you preventing God's answering. That can be so much hurtful, cruel nonsense at times. The answer may be spiritual, cosmic malevolence on a fearsome level that is causing delay, but never defeat! Taking this perspective maturely may be much more helpful and productive than other, more immature and cruel accusatory alternatives may be.

Paul: It Is Enough?

When the Apostle Paul tells us that he prayed three times for a "thorn in the flesh" to leave him before he got that memorable answer, "My grace is sufficient for you, for my power is made perfect in weakness" (2 Cor 12:9), it is impossible to tell what the precise time frame was. Did he mean that he prayed three times in the space of the same prayer? Did he mean that he prayed this same prayer on different days, or over the course of weeks, or months even? We are just not told. In one sense it doesn't matter. For at least two times of praying for deliverance from this thorn he got no answer. Or at least, let us imagine that is the correct interpretation. Of course, he could mean that after each of the three times he got the same answer. Again, it makes no real difference to my point in choosing this testimony.

My reason for selecting it is this: it harks back to something I have already touched on. When we want something o badly, and when we think we have good reason to pray for it, we just assume the answer is the one we want. That may well have been Paul's assumption. The part that precedes this testimony reveals something of the incredible spiritual experiences given to Paul. The whole purpose of the apostle's argument at this stage in the letter had been to respond to a group of Christians at Corinth who were boasting about their advanced levels of spiritual encounter as a way of demeaning the authority of the apostle. The culture in Corinth was very much an honor-based one, where it was important to outdo the next man or woman. Boasting, therefore, was endemic! However, it should never be so with the Christian. On the contrary, the Christian culture is one of honor in weakness. So why was Paul boasting? Only as a way of putting down those who were trying to humiliate him and to depose him as an apostle. Thus, he chose to boast only as a last resort, and only because he gloried in a different kind of boasting, admitting his own weakness (2 Cor 11:30). Therefore, it was with great regret that he called upon his own advanced spiritual experience and encounters with God as he did (12:1–5). But that encounter with God ensured his sense of personal weakness was never to be forgotten, because of this "thorn in the flesh" (12:5–10). Two things, in fact, guaranteed his weakness: one was the thorn in the flesh; the other was his utter dependency upon God's grace for the thorn leaving him or for the ability to cope with it if it didn't leave. That dependency upon God involved prayer. In the end, he got an answer. It was "No . . . but . . . ," or "No, the thorn will not leave you," as the implicit answer; "*but*, my grace is sufficient for you, for my power is made perfect in weakness," as the explicit answer. I don't know how easy it was for Paul to accept that, at least at first. Again, there are two possible perspectives. If he got that answer after the first attempt, then maybe the fact that he asked again, and again, is indicative that he did not accept it easily at first. If he did not get any reply after the first two attempts, it may indicate he was always hoping, and assuming, the Lord would take the thorn away, so he could serve God unhindered by it.

Whatever was the perspective of Paul, I suggest this incident may proffer help to others of us who most definitely find coping with delayed answers to prayer for urgent needs a problem. This is my main reason for choosing this testimony of Paul the Apostle.

We do not know what the "thorn in the flesh" was. Commentators have speculated, based on various bits of information about Paul's struggles and health issues hinted at in his letters. However, absolutely nothing can be decided conclusively, nor does our purpose require a decisive conclusion. Whether this thorn represented some clinical disease, or some psycho-spiritual struggle, or a relational struggle, we don't know. It was more than likely one of these. Assuming this to be the case makes this testimony useful for us.

The fact is, as an example of how messy and uncomfortable life can really be, Christians do sometimes have to live with disquieting clinical diagnoses of illness, or with psychological problems, or with relational struggles. What is more, these have a way of prompting Christians to pray earnestly about them—for some guidance and direction, for some understanding, for healing even—and nothing may come in return for those prayers, or so it seems. Little can be so distressing for anxious souls as this outcome.

One possible, and credible, interpretation of this passage is to conclude from it that the promise of God's grace being assuredly sufficient for those who must live with their clinical disease, or with their psychological or relational struggle, is applicable for all Christians at times. So, though the Apostle Paul needed this point to be brought home to him in an immediate manner—for that seems to be the inference from his testimony, "He said to me . . ." (v. 9)—it is enough for the rest of us to deduce this from the scriptural record of those words given to Paul. We don't get the *direct* word, in other words. Now, that may be where we should leave the matter, for, after all, there are many lessons we learn from Scripture that were, originally, given directly to one or another person or group of persons, for our benefit (e.g., 1 Cor 10:11). The difficulty arises when we take a slightly different line to Paul's testimony, but a no less credible one. We could also take the testimony to be more prescriptive. That is, we could take the fact of Paul's anxiety being so acute that he felt compelled to pray three times for the thorn to leave followed by getting that promise of sufficient grace in return, to be how it should be for us when we pray so earnestly and out of such anxiety. We too should expect God to say something directly to us in return. The fact is that it doesn't happen all the time, or even most of the time. Most times we have to interpret the answer, indirectly, out of Scripture. In such distressing and, at times, pressing circumstances, "Why can't we hear something direct, just for us?" seems an understandable request for those who have a friend in Jesus.

One answer could be that, now, once the full canon of Scripture has been given, there is no further need for such immediate speech from God. Don't forget, what Paul describes of his experience in 2 Cor 12 was exceptional even by his own standards—something he experienced by virtue of being lifted up to the "third heaven" (v. 2). It was an extraordinary encounter with God, so much so that it served Paul's purposes of boasting because it was so exceptional and beyond anything he believed his "competitors" could come up with (v. 11). So much of what we understand about God's will and purpose is now derived from Scripture, not from direct words from God. This is one reason why Bible study and expository ministry and the traditions of the church are so important for Christians now. These represent the voice of God for today's answers to prayer.

Certainly there is much truth in this perspective. One wonders how much prayer goes "unanswered," in the perception of some, because they don't make use of the means God has designed for hearing his answers. Imagine Christians who never read 2 Cor 12, but who move in Christian circles where guidance by direct revelation is plugged. Imagine they increasingly and desperately pray for some "thorn" in their flesh to be removed and become utterly disheartened when it isn't, though the answer is already there in 2 Cor 12 and they could be content in it! Waiting for God to respond in direct speech can never be an excuse for getting upset about unanswered prayer when the Scriptures so often speak directly to our prayers. In this redemptive relationship God has ordained the means by which the relationship is best conducted, and certainly it is the means of Scripture in conjunction with conscious involvement with the Holy Spirit that is the most prescribed means.

Conclusion

These accounts of prayer, which can, to different degrees, be construed as saying something on unanswered prayer, reveal a variety of general points for addressing the problem. Whether it's a matter of giving more seriousness to prayer, accepting "no" for an answer, exercising patience during delays, recognizing the cosmic conflict, or living with the problem but having grace sufficient for coping with it, we would do well to learn and apply these points in the interpretation of whether our prayers are being unanswered or not.

5

Heartbreaking Prayer

Having reflected on specific passages within Scripture that have some bearing on the problem of unanswered prayer, it is time to draw together some theological and pastoral observations. We need to consider these biblical reflections to see if they can contribute to a more substantial, practical theology of prayer, one that takes into account some of the pastoral problems we have already introduced.

By all accounts, the prophet Habakkuk was impressive. Amid his seriously felt confusion regarding what God was doing in his day, in using the wicked Chaldean nation to punish his own covenant people, he prayed about it and resolved to take himself off to the "watchpost," to wait for an answer (Hab 2:1). But what does that mean for us today?

In his popular commentary on Habakkuk, the late Martyn Lloyd-Jones, reflecting on this resolve of the prophet, makes a pastoral comment that, in my mind, has a helpful and yet, if we are not careful, unreal point to it. He says, "But the important consideration is that Habakkuk now realizes that the one thing to do is to wait upon God. It is not enough just to pray, to tell God about our perplexities, and just to cast our burden on the Lord. We must go further and wait upon God." I agree with Lloyd-Jones absolutely on that! All too often Christians say a prayer and then move on hurriedly to something else entirely different—so many prayers being made, and then forgotten! There is no "waiting." Now, Lloyd-Jones' pastoral comment, which he proceeds to stress, could be mistaken to mean he endorsed such a practice. He says of the prophet's approach,

> Now here is one of the most important principles in the psychology of the Christian life, or the understanding of how to fight in the spiritual conflict. Once we have taken a problem to God, we should cease to concern ourselves with it. We should turn our backs upon it and centre our gaze upon God.... We have a perplexity, and we have applied the prophetic method of laying down postulates and putting the problem in the context of those propositions which we have laid down. But we still do not find satisfaction, and we do not quite know what to do. It may be the problem of what we are to do with our lives; or it may be some situation that is confronting us which involves a difficult decision. Having failed to reach a solution, despite seeking the guidance of the Holy Spirit, there is nothing more to do but to take it to God in prayer.[1]

Then he presses his point again, that we should not continue to worry about the problem because it amounts to unbelief and wasted prayer if we do.[2] He also affirms that we should then expect an answer, and watch and wait for an answer. Now, he makes a valid point. It is wrong for such a pray-er to continue to fret in a state of unbelieving anxiety, once he or she has placed the issue in God's hands. My concern with what the "Doctor" says is that it doesn't make enough of what constitutes such a prayer of faith in the first place. He does refer to the prophet's perplexity, but he misses the fact that all that perplexity was expressed in direct communion with God. Lloyd-Jones comments in terms of principles and propositions, but he neglects this aspect of the prophet turning over his confusion in the very presence of God himself. It is my contention that many Christians struggle with unanswered prayer as they perceive it, because they do not enter into the struggle of prayer enough, and so end up doing the very thing Lloyd-Jones advises against: they "then forget about it."[3] Prayers are too easily made—and can, therefore, be too easily forgotten! So, allow me to enlarge where the "Doctor" didn't.

I cannot understand why any Christian, or Christian church, can live comfortably with unanswered prayer. Don't misunderstand me: I don't mean living with an active practice of faith in God's providential care. That must surely be the norm for the Christian, since "the righteous shall live by his faith" (Hab 2:4). That was how Habakkuk was to live in regard to the strange will of God in his day, and I shall return to emphasize this point,

1. Lloyd-Jones, *From Fear to Faith*, 36–37.
2. Ibid.
3. Ibid., 39.

specifically in regard to prayer. For now, I mean that kind of comfort, or ease, which seems oblivious to how much prayer has gone unanswered. Yet many live in such ease. If the truth be known, we all do, more than we think. For those who keep a record of those petitions they have made in their prayers, perhaps it is a little less likely than for those who don't keep up such a practice for very long. Philip Yancey, who, it seems, does keep, and review, a record of his intercessory prayers, tells us that his own emphasis in prayer has moved "from petition to compassion," and so he no longer agonizes over unanswered prayer as much as he used to.[4] That may be because he does keep a check on his petitions when he makes them. However, I would guess this would not represent many of us who, as Christians, have prayed and asked the Lord for so much that we have forgotten the better part of it—unless, that is, it has been those petitions that have come from our most broken or most passionate hearts at the time. Then such petitions do tend to stick in the memory, because they mean so much to *us*. As regards the rest of our prayerful requests to God, we just don't review the record, to see if there has been an answer or not.

A most helpful book I once read drew my attention to the importance of this point of Christians having an obligation of grace to deliberately look out for God to answer their prayers. The Puritan theologian and pastor Thomas Goodwin wrote a book titled *The Return of Prayers*; early on, he states the main point of the book: "The main observation and subject of this discourse thence deduced: That God's people are diligently to observe the answers to their prayers."[5] He then sets out the main reasons as to why this should be: that to neglect this is to take the ordinance of prayer in vain; God's attributes will be taken in vain; if we don't listen out for answers we let God speak to us in vain; we shall not be thankful and bless God for answers when they come; we shall lose our comfort. Any one of these reasons surely is sufficient to maintain looking for answers to prayer is important; but taking all together makes the case unassailable. God's glory depends on it!

Unlike Habakkuk, so many of us today do not *watch* and *wait* for the return of prayer. Alternatively, we just live with a "due proportionality" approach to prayer. That is, we accept that in our broadcasting of prayer, much of what we "send up to God in prayer" will not register, but a proportion must get through. So, we settle for the proportion and accept a good degree of "natural wastage." As long as *some* prayer gets answered—enough

---

4. Yancey, *Prayer*, 208.
5. Goodwin, *Return of Prayers*, Kindle location 25.

to satisfy us that God is alive and that he cares—the rest can go the way of all unanswered prayer, as it were. However, prayer is meant to come from belief that God *is* faithful, not as a test of *whether or not* he is.

For some, whose interest and experience of prayer is more ritualistic, just saying the words of set prayers or written liturgies can be what it is all about. This is in no wise to imply that the use of written prayers or of a liturgy is wrong or deficient for true prayer. My point is only to comment on some for whom the written liturgy becomes a kind of mantra. Their end is not to have specific prayers answered, but to achieve some kind of divine protective comfort for themselves and others they care about. It is worth my saying that such praying can also be a device that those who suffer from an obsessive compulsive disorder (OCD) can resort to for their psychological comfort. For those trapped in this cage of fear—for such OCD most surely is—then prayer can be a psychological ritual, perhaps a defense against the trauma of some earlier crisis. Answers are irrelevant unless something goes horribly wrong. The times of prayer, getting the precise forms of prayer right, and the associated rituals, are far more meaningful than answers. For those victims of such a disorder I feel very deeply—having been there myself, many years ago. However, prayer is not designed as a healthcare utility. Prayer as it should be—as an integral part of a living relationship with God through Christ as one's Savior and Lord—can be the means of a total release from the trap of OCD, a release into a vital relationship with God where real communion and answers matter in a relationship of freedom, not of entrapment. Prayer as it shouldn't be can be a mere psychological utility for the self.

But my key point is this: living while loaded with the backlog of so much unanswered prayer ought to disturb us Christians much more than it does. At worst, being content with unanswered prayer can betray a lack of real relationship. Integral to significant relationships are communication and reciprocity—speaking to one another, two-way communication. When that breaks down, on either side, it is at least a sign that something may be wrong. Will two lovers feel content if one of them senses that the other is not speaking to them as much, or is not there where they usually meet, or when gaps of time widen between sending and receiving letters? For a Christian to play indifferent when her prayers are not answered is a sign of a relationship with God in trouble, I suggest. Love will not tolerate indifference and forgetfulness. Even when it appears that this is how God has become—indifferent—lovers of God will not resign themselves easily.

They will pester their Love until he tells them why he seems to be so silent: What's gone wrong? What have I done? Why don't you answer? These will be heartfelt questions. If the Song of Songs is a dramatic depiction of true love between lovers (which pretty well every Christian thinks), and also between Christ and his church (which some Christians think), then the importance of intimate communication is unquestionable, from a biblical perspective. A breakdown in communication between lovers raises fears of distancing, and maybe of an impending breakup. Where a Christian has been attracted to that divine Lover by virtue of his promises of unfailing love and faithfulness, which *that Lover* has made the first move on (1 John 4:10)—where their relationship has been built upon such commitments—then who will sit quietly if the lack of answers seems to betray those commitments and stirs thoughts of an impending desertion and heartbreak? What we would never tolerate in our human relations of love, we seem to accept in our relationship with God. Such coolness at the prospect of being distanced from God! Where has the restlessness and heartbreak gone out of our prayers in response to the divine silence? I suggest that these should also be integral features of our active waiting upon God for answers to our prayers. They are sanctioned by Scripture.

6

Lament

READ AGAINST THE BACKCLOTH OF our brief theology of God-ness in chapter 1, and, as we closed the previous chapter, of prayer as a relationship of love, unanswered prayer should provoke more impatience than it seems it does for many of us in the Christian community. Is that right, though? Isn't patience a Christian virtue, after all? At the root of the Greek word sometimes translated as "patience" in the New Testament is actually the concept of perseverance, holding up under the strain, so to speak, or "hanging in there," as we say today. It is not a concept, therefore, that demands utter passivity, a kind of Buddhist submission. It can be very active in searching out means, and reasons, to persevere. It can be activity that borders on impatience, in fact.

Should there really be more impatience on our part in this matter? The very suggestion can seem absurd, even blasphemous, I grant you. How can the saved-from-so-much get impatient with their Savior? What possible grounds could sinners, with such natural self-interest, small minds, and meager comprehension, have for becoming impatient with a God whose thoughts, ways, and timing are clearly very different from our own (Isa 55:8–9)? However, the question remains, for built into the theology of God and prayer seems some biblical warrant for impatience in the face of unanswered prayer, at least enough to warrant a brief exploration of an intriguing feature called lament.

In the Old Testament there is a category of psalms that theologians call psalms of lament. Some of these are corporate in nature—laments by the whole gathered community—and some are individual, personal. Either way, a cluster of these are concerned with God's not answering prayer. Some examples may help shed light. Psalm 10, for instance, begins, "Why, O Lord, do you stand far away? Why do you hide yourself in times of trouble?" Now, that was asked in the context of a man of God experiencing a kind of atheistic onslaught from the "wicked," which represented a crass injustice into which crisis the psalmist had hoped for God to intervene. That God had not as yet intervened was a surprise to the psalmist, in view of the character of God as he understood it (vv. 12–18). So, he made this cry of impatience in a prayer to the Lord. Then there is Ps 13, with the repeated, anguished plea "How long?" coming four times in a short but earnest prayer, and a call for an answer (v. 3). The repetition of "How long?" reveals a soul that has been waiting repeatedly for an answer. In Ps 22 this despair over God's "silent treatment" comes across strongly again: "O my God, I cry by day, but you do not answer" (v. 2). The psalmist is conscious of being seen as someone for whom God did not answer prayer, which only heightened his despair: "All who see me mock me; . . . 'He trusts in the Lord; let him deliver him'" (v. 8); he implies that God's silence would bring additional mockery from unbelievers. This cry is, of course, now made so much more evocative since it became the cry of Jesus, as, dying on the cross, he experienced the mocking of the spectators and God's silence (Matt 27:42–46). Take Ps 35 as yet another instance. In the face of injustice toward him from certain enemies, the psalmist appeals, "You have seen, O Lord; be not silent! O Lord, be not far from me! Awake and rouse yourself for my vindication, for my cause, my God and my Lord" (vv. 22–23). In fact, in Ps 44 this appeal for God to wake up from his apparent sleep is put in a much stronger form: "Awake! Why are you sleeping, O Lord? Rouse yourself! Do not reject us forever!" (v. 23). In a prayer that depicts the emotional roller coaster of faith, the author of Ps 69 passes from a confidence in waiting for the Lord's own time to answer his prayer to becoming increasingly distressed and demanding: "Answer me, O Lord, for your steadfast love is good" (v. 16). But the darkest and most despairing of all pleas comes with the experience recorded in Ps 88. This represents, from beginning to end, a cry for prayer to be answered: "O Lord, God of my salvation; I cry out day and night before you. Let my prayer come before you; incline your ear to me!" (v. 1); "But I, O Lord, cry to you; in the morning my prayer comes before you. O Lord, why do you cast my soul away? Why do you hide your face from me?" (vv. 13–14).

Lament

So, what are we to make of these psalms? A number of points come to mind: first, the struggle over unanswered prayer is nothing new. This is not a modern phenomenon that has come into existence with the advent of a more advanced, scientific, modernist worldview, which must make prayer inevitably more difficult for modern, thinking people, especially when their world is so much faster moving and demanding of quick response. The fact is, Christians have struggled over this problem of unanswered prayer for millennia. Second, it is an experience that has brought Christians to occasional deep despair. There has never been an era when Christians have got this issue all sewn up and worked out. But here is a third point, and one that deserves a small diversion for a moment. *We have God's permission to express the despair we feel to him.*

This is the essence of lament, of course. Lament is a frank expression of confusion and hurt to God, even when the prime cause of that confusion and hurt seems to be God himself. We are allowed to say it like it feels! Lament refuses to present carefully crafted, duly censored prayers because they are made to God. All restraints are lifted in lament—it comes out like it feels inside. There is no "I need to be careful what I say because God might become angry or offended, or he may not be able to cope with it." It is OK to shout, "Answer me!" when he goes silent. It is allowed, because God has sanctioned it in his word. More impatience is endorsed, therefore! Without this impatience the impression can be given by Christian people that our prayers were just not that important to us after all. It can seem as if we prefaced them all with the words, "Not that urgent, but if and when you have time, if you want, should you be able to get round to it, Lord . . ." Or we just add the bland, "If it be Thy will," and leave it at that: prayer done and dusted, move on.

Now, a response to this cluster of laments might be, "But that is Old Testament teaching; that is how it was permitted then, when folk had much less revelatory light than in this New Testament era." Today, we should be more grown up in our praying. If prayers go unanswered then we should be big enough in our faith to just wait and trust—that is the impression Lloyd-Jones' perspective could easily give, though I am sure he would not have intended it. So, the unanswered prayers just stack up, all in the name of a "mature" waiting game. I am afraid I do not feel too much sympathy with such "maturity." In fact, I am very uncomfortable with it. Why?

Well, because, first of all, those Old Testament laments are a part of the hymnbook of the Old Testament church, and no less so of the New

Hello? Is Anyone There?

Testament church. Since when has the Christian church been asked to censor the Psalms in the name of maturity?! They are the only absolutely Holy Spirit–inspired hymns we have, with due respect to each and every subsequent hymn and spiritual songwriter that has come along since. It is, in my view, one of the most serious errors of the contemporary church that she places such a focus upon songs of praise and worship (so-called) and has almost ignored songs of lament. There is now hardly room in our modern or postmodern corporate worship for complaint to the Lord, for the church to lift up her corporate voice and shout, "WHY do you not hear our prayers? HOW LONG do we have to wait for you to answer?! AWAKE!" I cannot recall the last time I heard such a corporate plea in the context of worship.

I suggest strongly, therefore, that lament should become an integral part of our worship: it is allowed, sanctioned by God, in regard to our experiences of suffering, confusion, anger, despair, and unanswered prayer, which are commonplace experiences among God's people today. That we make little use of such lament in our worship, private and public, individual and corporate, is not *more* biblical or spiritual, but *less* than we are invited to express.

Without this dimension of lament, in the contemporary context of the Western church, and with the wholesale emphasis upon praise, one could be forgiven for thinking the issue of unanswered prayer is not an issue for today's Christian—that we are all too mature and incredibly strong in faith! Either the issue doesn't exist, or, if it does, it does not represent a problem. I beg to differ. The issue does exist—just talk to any praying Christian today in the Western world and, when honesty and frankness prevail over triumphalism, you will soon learn of the many who live, or rather struggle to live, with unanswered prayer. The sad thing is, for too many it doesn't disturb them enough—not enough to break the heart, or to break the mold of a routine of praise in favor of serious engagement in lament. For those who are disturbed by it, the current evangelical praise and worship culture can ensure lament is taboo. Like the comic John Cleese's classic line "Don't mention the War," we imply "Don't mention you're struggling!" during worship. This echoes our cultural triumphalist mood; so only the brave, or daft, dare to admit to struggling with the anguish of unanswered prayer. How alien this culture is to that of the Old and New Testament church, as her Spirit-inspired hymnbook makes clear.

Perhaps we don't get the answers to prayer we would wish, simply because we do not relate with the heartache and passion we ought to our heavenly Father. Let us not confuse reverence with spiritual prudishness. Perhaps honesty, the way it feels, is precisely what God is waiting to hear from us. However, to lament well we have first to properly engage with God.

7

Engaging with God

WHEN WE REFLECTED UPON JACOB'S encounter, his wrestling with the Angel of the Lord, in chapter 4, the point was made about prayer being serious. Jacob was, at many times in his life, never serious about God or others. He would seek to manipulate both to serve his own interests, hence the reason for the Lord coming to Jacob more as adversary than advocate. Rather than God being regarded as a fail-safe resource for getting out of a hole in life, it was time for Jacob to understand that messing with God was not a good idea or a lasting resource. Peniel was a test to see how much Jacob wanted to really engage with God more than with himself.

In fact, Abraham Kuyper, the late Dutch politician and theologian, when he wrote on the need for Christians to first seek and find God prior to engaging in making prayer, invoked both Isa 1:15, "When you spread out your hands I will hide my eyes from you; even though you make many prayers I will not listen," and Lam 3:44, "you have wrapped yourself with a cloud so that no prayer can pass through." He explained, "Scripture repeatedly shows us, therefore, that not every prayer counts as such with God. . . . Then the heaven is as brass; then there is no opening and no unlocking; there is no access and no entrance; and there is no grace and supplication."[1] In this meditation, Kuyper reflected, very practically, on how many families in the past, suffering from want of space and privacy, would go into a church building (which would be left open for such public access) to pray. People

---

1. Kuyper, *To Be Near unto God*, 337.

Engaging with God

would be proactive in finding space to pray. This resort of open church buildings, even for those who would wish it nowadays for their wrestling matches in prayer, has been denied us. Now most church buildings are locked except for church service days. But the point being made echoes that which Jesus made, when he taught his disciple how to pray: "When you pray, go into your room and shut the door and pray to your father who is in secret" (Matt 6:6). For want of us Christians, with our busy schedules, having the discipline, and the resolve for time and space to seriously engage with God as God, we can mistake an unanswered prayer for a non-prayer, if serious engagement is anything to go by. We can't wrestle with God in prayer in just a few minutes.

When, at first, prayers are not answered as soon as we would wish, and, in fact, prayer is hard work and struggle with nothing to show for it from the mouth of God, it is not beyond the bounds of possibility that, just as was the case for Jacob, God has become our adversary, just to see how much we want *him* and his blessing as our answer more than wanting him as a device for giving us what we want.

Another reason I am not happy with this fake "maturity" I previously alluded to is that it ignores key emphases in the New Testament teaching regarding prayer, which actually forewarns prayer *can* be unanswered and problematic, for a time at least. In Luke 11:5–13 Jesus drew on a scene in order to make the comparison between basic human instincts, of kindness and commitment, and those instincts of God. Well, in Luke 18:1–5, Jesus uses a somewhat similar, but not identical, scenario to assure Christian pray-ers concerning the commitment of God to dealing out justice. There is a significant difference from the Luke 11 scenario, however. In Luke 11 the thing that prevailed for the awakened neighbor was friendship and persistence, while in Luke 18 it is nagging! In the Luke 18 scenario there is no friendship. The awakened judge fears neither God nor man, but he cannot cope with being constantly nagged by the woman. What is interesting about this particular teaching is that it is intended to inspire perseverance in prayer so that one doesn't lose heart (v. 1). But how could the possibility of losing heart arise? By the fact that the early acts of prayer may not be answered as soon as one would hope. The method endorsed by Jesus is this: we are, as it were, to pester God, to be unrelenting about the lack of answers! I am reminded at this point of the prophet Isaiah, who, when instructing the watchmen who kept guard over the walls of Jerusalem, told them that they were to "take no rest" in putting the Lord in remembrance of what needed to be done to establish his glory in Jerusalem (62:6); but, more astonishingly, they were to "give him [the Lord] no rest" (62:7). The reason for the persistence would be that the Lord could have given all appearances of taking his rest by not answering the prayers of his people. For similar reasons some psalms, as we have seen, urge God to wake up.

Dare I say it, but getting *no* answer to our prayers should not be an option we accept easily in our serious engagement with God. Yet, having said that, I realize it is a statement capable of immense misunderstanding; so, important caveats are essential. I am not overlooking the fact that sometimes God answers our prayers, but not with the answer we want. That is not unanswered prayer then, and it amounts to peevishness to suggest it is. Nor am I thinking that in answering our prayer the Lord is obliged to give us every detail we think we require for it to be a proper, sufficient answer. After all, Job was at times most demanding of God to spell out the precise reasons for all the catastrophic traumas that his providence had allowed in Job's life. Job's laments and complaints were blunt (and to his pious "friends" seemed irreverent). Yet, God never answered Job's prayer—not in the way he expected or wished; there was no detail. There was just the divine presence made known to Job, and that was his answer. It was also enough!

But Job's case is of interest for another reason, not unrelated to perseverance. His experience presents another aspect of God as adversary, in fact. Job feared God had become his adversary, at least during the troughs of his despair (Job 7:12–21; 16:11–14). But no one can conclude, having read the book, that like Jacob, Job needed some sinful characteristics within him sorted out. Indeed, that was the perspective for which, in the end, God passed judgment on his friends (Job 42:7). Job never got an answer to those aspects of his prayerful laments, other than the revelation of God given to him in the whirlwind, satisfying him that what he did not know could not overwhelm the glory he did know after that revelation experience.

The point I am making is this: serious engagement and patient perseverance in prayer, which is endorsed so strongly in Scripture, is not the same as putting strong feelings of struggle on hold—thinking that because we are in God's presence, we should engage a stoicism that ensures we are all calm. Before I ever read the book of Job I heard people speak of the "patience of Job." That is how the King James Version translates the original word. Contemporary versions tend to translate it as "steadfastness" (ESV). When I read Job, as I have done many times, I don't see a lot of patience in him, not in the way we often associate that term: a sense of calm restraint that just waits and waits, brushes aside any strain and stress, and resists complaining. What I read in Job is huge stress, turbulence, and impatience. Job cannot understand why God has brought about so much pain and loss in his life, devastating his family, his livelihood, and his whole social sphere. Neither can he accept the multiple explanations given by his friends, nor the silence from God. He protests his innocence both to the friends and to God. He gets angry, he despairs, he weeps and he argues. But through it all he perseveres; he keeps asking, seeking, knocking, hoping, and believing. He will not give in to unbelief. His problem is not with any temptation toward atheism, brought about by pain and unanswered prayer; his problem is powerful theism, unabated belief in the mercy of God as creator and friend, but a friend turned apparent adversary. Determination to find the friendly face of God again was what produced the turbulence.

Many years ago I was preaching at a church in South Wales. I cannot remember what my text was, to be honest—it may well have been Isa 62:6–7. I do remember, though, choosing a particular hymn for that service. It was written by a man called Henry Twells, and it began with the words, "Awake, O Lord, as in the time of old!" For me it has always been a powerful hymn of desire for God. At the end of that service, however, one of the longstanding deacons of that church came to me and remonstrated with my choice of that hymn. He could not understand how Christians could sing, or pray, asking God, of all persons, to wake up. To be honest, in the light of all the confirmation Scripture gives us of God's omnipotence, and his never needing sleep, it can, indeed, seem an absurd if not irreverent thing to do. Yet it is entirely scriptural, for the prophet Isaiah uses the same expression: "Awake, awake, put on strength, O arm of the LORD; awake, as in days of old" (Isa 51:9). If it seems that the Lord is sleeping and not answering prayer, we have warrant to be impatient. The theology of God, objectively absorbed, should not quench the experience of a relationship that has become subjectively confused, and the sense that God has gone to sleep on us. We Christians should not be easy to go to sleep on—we need to be those who keep up a persevering noise through the "nights" of unanswered prayer. In that helpful book *Don't Just Stand There . . . Pray Something!*, Ronald Dunn advises we pray until we receive an *answer*, until we receive *assurance* that we will receive an answer, or until God says, "No."[2] So, until any of these is fulfilled we have plenty of prayer work with which to engage with God. The issue of trust is a case in hand.

---

2. Dunn, *Don't Just Stand There*, 198–200.

8

Trust Me!

I am conscious there must be a balancing factor to my endorsement of turbulence in persevering in prayer if it is to be distinguished from faithless desperation. The Bible has such a balance in a further aspect of prayer brought out in Scripture—something to do with trust.

The Bible speaks of "waiting." That is an interesting term and concept, isn't it? What does it mean in the context of prayer? Does it mean Christians pray and then just sit around, perhaps drumming their fingers impatiently, waiting for an answer? Does it mean they pray, then put that prayer behind them, forget it, and sit patiently and stoically—or only return to the issue occasionally—waiting for an answer? What does it mean to "wait"?

In a classic passage that has to do with God's people feeling their prayers were unanswered—"Why do you say, O Jacob, and speak O Israel, 'Why is my way hidden from the Lord, and my right is disregarded by my God?'" (Isa 40:27)—the Lord reminds them of things they already had been made aware of in terms of God's character and provision. The people are reminded of God's everlastingness, his creatorship, his tirelessness, his understanding, his power. "Have you not known? Have you not heard? The Lord is the everlasting God, the Creator of the ends of the earth. He does not faint or grow weary; his understanding is unsearchable" (vv. 28–29). Then, while he acknowledges that the stressful circumstances the people were going through at that time were enough to exhaust the natural strength even of youths, nevertheless they need not exhaust God's people, irrespective of their age, if they "wait for the Lord." By "waiting" they will renew their strength: "Even youths shall faint and be weary, and young men shall fall exhausted; but they who wait for the Lord shall renew their strength; they shall mount up with wings like eagles; they shall run and not be weary; they shall walk and not faint" (vv. 30–31).

In fact, throughout the Old Testament, the same Hebrew word is translated sometimes as "wait" and sometimes as "hope." So there is a strong meaning of waiting in the sense of trusting. This ingredient is essential in prayer and in perseverance when prayer seems unanswered. In Ps 25 this equation of trust with waiting is expressed in the prayer of David; he begins, "To you, O Lord, I lift up my soul. O my God, in you I trust" (vv. 1–2), and then affirms, "Indeed, none who wait for you shall be put to shame" (v. 3). Then, later, he confesses, "May integrity and uprightness preserve me, for I wait for you" (v. 21). While desperate turbulence can lead to the loss of Christian integrity, "waiting," or trusting God, can ensure the highest level of integrity in a Christian. In Ps 27, a prayer bristling with trust in the face of the fear of not being heard, the psalmist affirms that he has sincerely sought the face of God in prayer and he wants the Lord to guide him. So, he counsels himself, "Wait for the Lord; be strong and let your heart take courage; wait for the Lord" (v. 14). In Ps 130, another context of hurt over apparent unanswered prayer, or fear that circumstances of personal sin could prevent prayer being answered, the author prays, "I wait for the Lord, my soul waits, and in his word I hope; my soul waits for the Lord more than watchmen for the morning, more than watchmen for the morning" (vv. 5–6). Given that prayer is made on the foundation of scriptural promises and directions, we need to follow up on our prayers with trustful hope in the validity of that foundation. It is such a promise-based foundation to our praying that prevents despair as the days, weeks, months, and even years roll by without an answer. Hope in the word of promise is what sustains us and prevents despair. This is what it is to "wait."

In other words, waiting is another way of describing faith; far from being the rather passive status we commonly associate with the word *wait*, the biblical sense is far from passive. It involves an active, sustained trust in God, which, in turn, sustains an active perseverance in prayer.

Sometimes, as I have been "waiting" for God to answer my prayers—especially if those prayers have been about changing some unhappy and uncomfortable circumstances—I have been rebuked for my impatient turbulence by remembering the case of the Old Testament patriarch Joseph. He had to endure years of suffering and misfortune—sold into slavery as a youth by his own brothers, wrongfully accused of attempted sexual assault, and being thrown into prison and forgotten, Joseph was then given hope by the prospect of a fellow prisoner mentioning him favorably to the pharaoh. But that hope was dashed as that prisoner just forgot all about Joseph for another two years before, at last, remembering and mentioning Joseph. You can read the drama in Gen 37–41. It is inconceivable to think that Joseph did not pray while undergoing such trials, year upon year of nothing happening. How did he cope? How did he hope for anything in that rotten prison confinement, feeling so forgotten, so let down? When people forget us it is so easy to feel as though God has forgotten us. Joseph gives us a hint when, some years later, as he is reunited with his repentant brothers, he comforts them with this truth: "And now do not be dismayed or angry with yourselves because you sold me here, for God sent me before you to preserve life. . . . So it was not you who sent me here, but God" (Gen 45:5, 8); and again, "As for you, you meant evil against me, but God meant it for good, to bring it about that many people should be kept alive, as they are today" (Gen 50:20). Something that is evil God can use for good—both our good and that of others.

The case of Joseph, in regard to unanswered prayer, presents us with some significant help; not least it holds before us the importance of some answers taking much longer than feels comfortable—and, if we are to cope with this fact, the absolute necessity of a passionate belief in God's providence that waiting is not a waste of our life. Often, looking back provides the most beautiful perspective on God's apparent silences!

While we are reflecting upon "waiting," perhaps we should also take into account the times when the psalmist cried out to God, "How long?" (e.g., Ps 13:1–2). There can be times in life when the most earnest and urgent prayers of our hearts seem to go unanswered; meanwhile, our hearts seem to break for waiting. It does not take much imagination to think of Joseph praying, "How long, Lord? How long?!" Every day, perhaps many times a day, all we can say in our prayer is "How long, O Lord?"

How do we cope with that kind of anguish? The psalmist helps us: "But I have trusted in your steadfast love." That is all we have to go on—God's steadfast love. Precisely because of that element of the Christian drama, it's not over until it's over. Keep praying—just you wait!

9

Delays and Providence

SOMETIMES I FEAR WE WESTERN Christians can create for ourselves, often out of our theology, an unreal, sanitized, less messy view of life; we see life as less complex than it truly is in the contemporary world, or was in biblical times. This is probably why we struggle as we do with evil and suffering, and with the problem of unanswered prayer. It is why we have unrealistic expectations, which surface in unreal prayers.

This was a lesson the friends of Job had to learn as they struggled to understand Job's actual state and his reaction to his unanswered prayers for help and explanation. These friends tried to protect themselves with their unreal theology of cause and effect. The alternative—reality—probably terrified them: that in the real world you could suffer so horribly even if you were righteous!

The prophet Habakkuk, also, had to learn a lesson from the messiness of life and prayer, living as he did during one of the most complex and turbulent periods of Old Testament history: when the Lord brought the Babylonians (Chaldeans) to conquer Judah, God's covenant people. For the prophet, this caused all kinds of theological and moral dilemmas, which he voiced in the book that takes his name. The main dilemma was how a covenant-keeping God could allow the violent and cruel Babylonian army to come and conquer God's own people. This was an issue the prophet had been praying about for a long time and got no answer to: "O LORD, how long shall I cry out for help and you will not hear?" (Hab 1:2). Notice, this was one of those "How long?!" prayers we referred to earlier. But it is his reaction that is interesting as well. He didn't give up in despair even though he did express his incredulity in frank terms: "Why do you make me see iniquity; and why do you idly look at wrong? Destructions and violence are before me; strife and contention arise" (1:3). Theologically and morally, he could not make any sense of the brief answer he did eventually receive:

> Look upon the nations, and see; wonder and be astonished. For I am doing a work in your days that you would not believe if told. For behold, I am raising up the Chaldeans, that bitter and hasty nation, who march through the breadth of the earth, to seize dwellings not their own. They are dreaded and fearsome; their justice and dignity go forth from themselves. Their horses are swifter than leopards, more fierce than the evening wolves; their horsemen press proudly on. Their horsemen come from afar; they fly like an eagle swift to devour. They all come for violence, all their faces forward. They gather captives like sand. At kings they scoff, and at rulers they laugh. They laugh at every fortress, for they pile up earth and take it. Then they sweep by like the wind and go on, guilty men, whose own might is their right. (1:5–11)

So, the prophet chose to stand at his "watch-post" and to wait and see how God would answer (2:1). The answer did come, eventually, in a fuller manner (2:6—3:19). This made it clear to the prophet that the Chaldeans were only acting under God's permission to enact the judgment the covenant people brought upon themselves for their own persistent and pernicious disobedience. However, God was also fully aware of the Chaldeans' arrogance and violence, and he would execute judgment upon them in due course—for their violent greed (2:6–8), their corruption (2:9–11), their violence (2:12–14), and their drunkenness and idolatry (2:15–20). This, in turn, stirred the prophet to respond in worship of the Lord, and, significantly, to a more patient and faithful waiting, as is expressed in his memorable affirmation at the end of the book:

> Though the fig tree should not blossom, nor the fruit be left on the vines, the produce of the olive fail and the fields yield no food, the flock be cut off from the fold, and there be no herd in the stalls, yet I will rejoice in the LORD, I will take joy in the God of my salvation. God, the Lord, is my strength; he makes my feet like the deer's; he makes me tread on my high places. (3:17–19)

Delays and Providence

So, here is trust in God, even when your nation, or business and livelihood, go to the wall—when no amount of prayer brings a rescue! How can that make sense? Habakkuk confesses in his prayer (3:1–16) that it was based on his trust in the providential will of God in regard to his purpose in using the Chaldeans. With his confidence in God's providence the prophet could "wait" for God to bring in the terrible "day of trouble" (3:16). It was tough, but it was possible.

Similarly, Joseph put his trust, during those darkest moments in prison, in God's providence, as did Jesus in the Garden of Gethsemane, where he agonized in prayer over the necessity of his going to the cross (Matt 26:39–42). A more recent example of trusting God in a time of great uncertainty can be found in the story of Jay, a foreign student who came to university to do his PhD, providing his own funding. This was very expensive for an overseas student, of course. As he approached the task of finally writing up his material, his supervisor delayed in reading and commenting on his chapters for so long—providing no explanation—that the three years he projected for the work stretched out into nearly six, with all the increases in costs he had to bear himself. His pastor used to urge him to protest more strenuously to the university, but each time he would say, "No—I know God is in control of this. I will trust him." Well, amid great rejoicing he finally graduated and returned home to apply for lecturing jobs, and to care for a sick parent. After some months of waiting on God he obtained a part-time post in a good university, which then became a full-time post just as he was diagnosed with cancer! Yet, through all the subsequent surgery and uncomfortable chemotherapy and radiotherapy, he continued to place his love and trust in God's providence, as he waited for his prayers to find an answer.

Such a scenario reminds us of the sheer hurt that can be invested in prayer, and when such prayer remains unanswered it hurts so much more.

So, what is this providence, and how does it serve us in addressing unanswered prayer? I like Professor John Webster's definition: providence is "that work of divine love for temporal creatures whereby God ordains and executes their fulfilment in fellowship with himself." Therefore, an actual doctrine of providence "is a conceptual meditation on the consolation and hope this work of love generates."[1] Providence is the reflection upon the way that God, in love for his people, has a purpose for the good of his people, and is sure to fulfill that in his own time. In practical theol-

---

1. Webster, "On the Theology of Providence."

ogy terms, it is summarized by the Apostle Paul in his conviction that "for those who love God all things work together for good, for those who are called according to his purpose" (Rom 8:28). Interestingly, that affirmation comes in the context of prayer. What had started the line of thought, for the apostle, was the Holy Spirit helping Christians in their weakness in regard to prayer. "For we do not know what to pray for as we ought, but the Spirit himself intercedes for us with groaning too deep for words" (8:26). Faced with severe life-and-death struggles, as Christians can be, prayer is not easy. Circumstances can be such that we just don't know what to pray for, or we are just too weak to pray for anything. So Paul reassures us that, under such dire conditions, the Spirit of God helps us by interceding for us with his perfect understanding of the will of God. So, sometimes, when we are praying, we just need to place the issues in the Spirit's hands and allow him to intercede for us—trusting that the will of God is always wanting, and working for, our good.

Now, that is tough faith! But it is critical faith in prayer. In essence, it confirms that if there *really is* anything like actual unanswered prayer, then it is rare. As we have noted, sometimes when a prayer is not genuine, then it is just a playing with motives and words God has said he will not answer. At other times the answer is "no." At still other times it is an answer in the process of coming to us—it is delayed, though we don't know for how long—or an answer we will not accept because it is hard for us, and only time will provide the necessary scope to come round to accepting it.

For people who like to be in control of their lives, as most of us are naturally inclined to be, not knowing is tough. But on what basis should it not be tough? Has *God* said it will not be tough? Do we deserve to have it easy? In fact, for it to always be easy we would have to have God be the servant of our wish to know all things, which he is not. Our business is to trust God, not to dictate to him or use him! Ours is to believe that God knows what is best for us, because he loves us. He knows what is best, and he knows the best time for us to have what is best. There is no better answer to the kind of experience C. S. Lewis graphically describes was his, while in the throes of grief, following the death of his wife from cancer. Lewis writes,

> Meanwhile, where is God? This is one of the most disquieting symptoms. When you are happy, so happy that you have no sense of needing Him, so happy you are tempted to feel His claims upon you as an interruption, if you remember yourself and turn to Him

Delays and Providence

with gratitude and praise, you will be—or so it feels—welcomed with open arms. But go to Him when your need is desperate, when all other help is vain, and what do you find? A door slammed in your face, and a sound of bolting on the inside. After that, silence. You may as well turn away. The longer you wait, the more emphatic the silence will become.[2]

Granted that Lewis wrote *A Grief Observed* while he was heartbroken by the loss of his wife, and his personal experience may not be a universal one, even so, Lewis's experience will not be unique, and neither will it be restricted to bereavement. Those who feel their significant prayers are not being answered will have very similar feelings of having God's door slammed in their face, followed by silence. Somehow, and no one is saying it is easy, we have to find trust in the one who has, apparently, slammed the door in our face; to trust that what is going on "behind those closed doors," of which we have no idea, is actually bearable because the one in there is working all things for our good. The time will come when that door will open and he will come out and explain, or at least reassure us. Just when that will be only God knows. Meanwhile, can we trust—as Joseph found he could; as Job struggled to, but did; as David did more easily; and as Paul did after his struggle in prayer? To be sure of any hope in doing so you will need a doctrine of providence that feeds off a doctrine of grace—grace being the burner that warms every action of God on behalf of a Christian. That is precisely the point the Apostle Paul was making in that statement in Rom 8:28, as the following verses make clear:

> And we know that for those that love God all things work together for good, for those who are called according to his purpose. [How do we know this?] For those whom he foreknew he also predestined to be conformed to the image of his Son [the purpose], in order that he might be the firstborn among many brothers. And those whom he predestined he also called, and those whom he called he also justified, and those whom he justified he also glorified [also the purpose]. (Rom 8:28–30)

Never forget that these words of profound doctrine were crafted for the pastoral benefit of praying Christians struggling with understanding the most awful forms of persecution and suffering.

So, providence is not about God's being a sovereign information service, some divine tour guide who is on hand when we wish him to be, to

---

2. Lewis, *Grief Observed*, 7.

sort out all the glitches in our life and to provide all the information we want when we want it. Thank and praise God he is not such, for if God were to grant us everything we asked for, what kind of world would this be? Farmers and tourists would be demanding opposite things for their enjoyment! Sports competitors would be vying with God as to who would win! Love-smitten romantics would be praying to persuade God to allow them to win the heart of the same person! God knows how many of our prayers are just plain daft and selfish. Only someone who is either evil or insane (or both) would grant every prayer we make. The "all things" God works "for the good" of those who love him are focused around conforming us to the image of Christ (Rom 8:29). As Professor Paul Helm concludes, therefore, "Not until all the events of a person's life have occurred, until that life has come to an end, could the contributory significance of any particular event or events be definitely assessed."[3] So whether we have immediate answers to prayer or not will not make the meaning of our life any clearer, nor must the want of such answers necessarily make our life more meaningless. The doctrine of providence is unworkable outside of a framework of faith and trust in God, and our life of prayer must operate within this framework or it will just be cheap, and also tormenting by its deception.

In his *Providence of God*, Helm anticipates life can be such, sometimes, where no pattern in God's purpose can be discerned. Times of unanswered prayer often feel like that. But, he asks, what of times that become "stamped by monotony, or by loss and adversity?" His answer is that we need to call then upon the wider framework of the doctrine of providence, depending upon "faith holding on to the fact of this framework when there is nothing else." Such was the outlook of both Job and Habbakuk, Helm reminds us.[4] They, along with many others since, had to learn the lessons of praying and waiting out the delays God's providence supervises.

---

3. Helm, *Providence of God*, 127.
4. Ibid., 127–28.

10

Providence, Drama, and Mystery

THERE IS MYSTERY IN THE Bible, on two accounts not to be confused. In the first place, there is the gospel as mystery. The classic statement of this comes in Ephesians 3. But this "mystery" is not a mystery as we usually understand that word today. It does not mean the gospel is shrouded or is confusing, hidden as a meaning within a meaning, so to speak. The Apostle Paul used the term to speak of a thing once hidden but now revealed. The gospel was once hidden in the signs and shadows of the Old Testament revelation, but it has now been fully revealed in the person of Jesus Christ. Furthermore, something else that lay hidden has now been revealed, and that is God's purpose for the gospel, namely, to bring this good news of Jesus to the whole Gentile world, not just to the Jews, so that God's glorious plan can be witnessed by the world and by the rulers and authorities in the heavenly places (Eph 3:8–10). This is the predominant meaning of "mystery" in the New Testament.

This is not the meaning I imply by my use of the term, however. I am using it in the usual sense—a phenomenon that we do not fully understand, something that contains features and content that elude our net of comprehension, something "we cannot get our heads around." Any doctrine of providence that does not also believe in such mystery is not honest to the Bible or to life in prayer. To come to terms with unanswered prayer we have to accept mystery, in this sense, in the Christian drama.

The lessons of prayer are not easy lessons. That is why God's grace allows us to lament as we struggle to learn the difference between having

Hello? Is Anyone There?

God as a slot machine where we just drop in the currency of our prayer and expect to walk away with what we want, or having God as our father and friend, to whose will we desire to freely submit come what may. Even though it *seems* prayer is a reflex every human being possesses, and exhibits in so many different ways as it is influenced by culture, tradition, religion, or habit, in fact prayer is God's gift whereby he invites us to relate with him in a reality that coexists happily with human responsibility. Prayer involves our responsibility of asking, seeking, knocking, persuading, and God's sovereignty—his right to govern as he wills, because he wills our good. For humans (and, dare I say it, for God) such relationships are never easy, but they represent significant aspects of the thrilling drama of redemption.

A *systematic* theological approach to the subject of prayer is often fraught with the methodology it is confined to—a system, in which one part dovetails with another and the resultant whole just about sums the subject up. But therein can be the problem: prayer has become a subject, or a system, more than a feature of a dramatic relationship. The concept of drama, therefore, in my mind, is much more suited to such a relationship. The system must never take precedence over the narrative, the plot, the big story, the unfolding drama, inclusive of mystery.[1]

Given this approach to the problem of unanswered prayer, the element of mystery is less difficult to live with. After all, we are quite at home with the concept of mystery in, for instance, dramatic presentations such as novels and films. In fact, that is their draw: we don't know the end from the beginning; we are not sure how the author will develop the plot, its subtle shifts and surprises, its twists and turns, how it comes to a climax, or how the characters will play their part in it. Some of us enjoy trying to work the plot out in advance, from clues along the way, hence the appeal of a good whodunit. But the awe hits when, come the finale, the author has managed to baffle us all with some kind of twist in the plot, something that was there all along but we just didn't see. That is what, in our view, makes for such an enthralling drama. In a sense the not knowing is the thing that keeps us enthralled. But reading or watching a drama in the comfort of our living room with the realization that it is only a story (fiction), or knowing it happened to someone else in the past (nonfiction), is a lot easier than you or I actually being actors in a live drama! There are some similarities, however. For example, as Christians we do not write the script, nor are we

---

1. For a comprehensive model of the Scriptures as drama, with Christ at the center as chief actor, see Vanhoozer, *The Drama of Doctrine*.

Providence, Drama, and Mystery

privy to all its details, or even in possession of absolute clarity as regards the full and final plot. God is the author; the Holy Spirit is the director; and Jesus Christ is the main actor. We too are actors, but never the main ones. The plot does not revolve around you and me; it all revolves around Jesus and for the glory of God. This is why there must always be an element of mystery about this drama, as far as we are concerned—in fact, in some aspects, even as far as Jesus was concerned (Mark 13:32). So, there will be limitations on any "faith seeking understanding" exercise. Even "faith seeking understanding" must, from time to time, confess with Job, "Behold, I am of small account: what shall I answer you? I lay my hand on my mouth" (Job 40:4), bow in reverent silence, and wait out the mystery. How much more worthy of awe is God than an Agatha Christie or a Steven Spielberg! How much more enthralling it can be to be an actor in God's drama—not watching, but taking part!

So, can we build into our prayer life the following understanding: "I haven't a clue what is going on; but I know and trust the One who does. I don't know the answer, but I know the Answerer"? Such an attitude could prevent panic and anxiety, and the wrong sort of persistent asking and nagging inquiry, or a crumbling of faith.

It is not by accident that Jesus, having spoken of prayer, how and how not to pray, in his Sermon on the Mount (Matt 6:1–15), then speaks of anxiety (6:25–34). In between those two he touches on the struggle concerning where our treasures are, and the need to store up treasure in heaven and to serve one master (6:19–24). I would suggest that a significant part of the problem we have with unanswered prayer lies in our struggle at this level. We hope that God is someone who will serve us and provide for us the treasure we want. So fixated upon this can we become that we are consumed with anxiety: will God come up with the goods, and if he doesn't who will, and what will we do if we can't have that treasure? What is more, we feel we need to know the answer to this from day to day, in advance even! The more time passes without our knowing, the more anxious we become. In fact, the principle Jesus lays down demands a contentment with *not* knowing the future: "Your heavenly father knows that you need [these things]. But seek first the kingdom of God and his righteousness and all these things will be added to you" (6:32–33). So there it is: we do not know; but we trust the One who does, the Answerer. That is a fundamental ground rule for all actors involved in this divine drama! Furthermore, there may be elements in what we do not know that we shall never—and I mean really, eternally—never know.

Has it ever struck you as intriguing that amid all the revelation of the second law in Deuteronomy (for that is what the word *deuteronomy* literally means in Greek, after the Greek Septuagint version of the Old Testament) and the renewing of the covenant with God, we have a word of caution about how to interpret that revelation?

In Deut 29 we have an account of the words spoken by God through Moses to the people of Israel at Moab, just prior to their entry into the promised land. They were reminded of all the Lord did for them while they were slaves in the land of Egypt, and the exodus out of Egypt, and their sojourn in the wilderness up to that point of their going into the land of promise. They were asked to enter into a covenant with the Lord again—a covenant renewal. A key aspect of that covenant was the warning against presuming on the grace of God with the thought, "I shall be safe, though I walk in the stubbornness of my heart" when they were tempted to commit idolatry (Deut 29:18–19). If the people chose to take that attitude, then the covenant would be broken and God's wrath would be incurred (vv. 20–28).

Now, that stood to raise theological problems for an Israelite, because, unlike the covenant made by other nations, God's covenant was established only on his terms. That was the only way to ensure salvation was by grace alone. If it was a covenant based on mutual terms, then it could never work because it would place a holy God and sinful humanity on an equal footing. That could not work. However, if the covenant was all of God and of his grace—his unmerited favor—*how could their sin break the covenant*? Thus, the whole issue of God's sovereignty and human responsibility was anticipated that early on in the history of theological and pastoral thought! That was why Scripture said, immediately following that warning, "The secret things belong to the Lord our God, but the things that are revealed belong to us and to our children forever, that we may do all the words of this law" (v. 29). Because the problem of unanswered prayer also touches on divine sovereignty and human responsibility, this statement is important for us to heed. It makes it clear that God has revealed all that we need to carry out our side of the covenant in regard to prayer, and it assures us that God is committed to carrying out his part in regard to our prayers as well. Just how these two concepts marry together is not revealed to us, so we do not need to know. However, it ensures mystery in providence, and this fact guarantees there will be times when we will not have a clue about what is going on. All we can do is trust and pray!

In our modern society and mindset there can be a real struggle with trusting God, whom we do not see and, in these cases, often do not understand. That militates against our post-Enlightenment pride, our trust in reason, our belief that if it is for real then science will be able to figure it out, make sense of it, or fix it so it can make sense. In fact, from a Christian perspective, from a biblical perspective, life is such that it has a certain quota about it that is designed never to be understood by us; creation has been designed that way, thus ensuring that if we will live in God's way, in relationship with him, as actors in the divine drama, we play substantial parts of our role by faith, by trust. The very way we enter the Christian life, through the gospel of Christ, insists on this (1 Cor 1:18–31), and the way we are to continue living this life requires the same levels of trust and faith. The key statement on the Christian life is simple: "The righteous shall live by faith" (Hab 2:4; cf. Rom 1:17). That is the principle that kept Habakkuk going in the face of so much that seemed to be inconsistent with God's justice and covenant love.

The resolution of the profound emotional struggle over unanswered prayer has to be some hard work of faith in just trusting God—accepting that, for the moment certainly, it might not make sense to you or me. If this were not so, then the drama we have been given the privilege to play a part in could be terribly predictable and boring. Contrary to so many secular rumors over the years—and, indeed, to the groaning of some of those who attend church services—*nothing* is ever boring with God, especially prayer! You just never know where prayer can lead: "The prayer of a righteous person has great power in its working. Elijah was a man with a nature like ours . . ." (Jas 5:16). That's why we read of his terrific struggles with God's not answering his prayers at times; that's why we read of his heartbreaking laments and anger. Yet, "he prayed fervently that it might not rain, and for three years and six months it did not rain on the earth. Then he prayed again, and heaven gave rain and the earth bore its fruit" (5:17–18)

I said at the outset that this would not be a book of anecdotes, to discourage spiritual voyeurism. I would like to make an exception at this particular juncture, however, in order to press home the thrilling point this chapter has majored on: the drama and mystery of living by trusting in the providence of God.

Hello? Is Anyone There?

There is a period in my own life that illustrates this well, I believe, if readers will bear with my relating it.

My wife, youngest daughter, and I recently returned from a memorable visit to Taiwan that I believe was a very clear answer to prayer made over a period of eight years or so—a period I felt was a great struggle with different prayers being unanswered for so much of the time.

I will spare you the details, but around nine to ten years ago a cluster of Taiwanese families came to our town to do postgraduate studies. They brought their children with them and this was how my wife first got to connect with them—through meetings at the local primary school, while delivering and returning children to and from school. Then, before long, some of these families started to attend services at our church, to show interest in Christianity and to ask for further instruction. We got to know them very well and we all became very good friends. Also, toward the end of this period one of the families had a father and sister from Taiwan, on holiday down in Cornwall, when news came of a close family bereavement back in Taiwan. I offered to drive the sister and her husband down to Cornwall quite late in the day to break this tragic news to the holidaying members of her family. I subsequently drove them all back later that night, and then the following day I took them to an airport for their return flight to Taiwan in connection with this family emergency. Shortly after this incident, about which I thought nothing other than being glad to be of some help, most of these Taiwanese families returned to Taiwan, their studies completed. Their departing from our town was quite a wrench for my wife and daughter, as they had become very close in their friendships. I could see this, and so I began to pray, concertedly, that God might allow me to take my wife and daughter to Taiwan one day to visit these friends. Of course, I had absolutely no idea how such a thing could happen, as airfares were way outside our finances.

What followed, over a period of around seven to eight years thereafter, was a time of unanswered prayer as I had never experienced in all my years as a Christian, and not just with reference to my prayers over visiting our friends in Taiwan; in fact, it had more to do with prayers around many other issues and incidents. There were many issues, some extraordinarily heartbreaking, that I was praying about—praying with as much sincerity as I could muster, praying with tears and groans. I can say before God: this was not praying for some wish list; it was not because I viewed God as being at my beck and call. No, these were issues that I felt his own glory

Providence, Drama, and Mystery

was involved in, his will. Year after year I kept up these prayers, as well as the prayers about Taiwan. In fact, at many points it seemed that God would come so close to answering my prayers on certain things. Many times he seemed to offer me glimmers and possibilities of those things I had prayed about for a long time, so much so that I couldn't help becoming excited at the prospect, only to then have the prospect dashed in some devastating way that consigned me back to the waiting process.

Then, in 2010, I got involved with an international organization that responds with Christian chaplains to scenes of major disaster—a field of work, it so happens, in which I was carrying out doctoral research at the time. I was deployed to the Caribbean nation of Haiti in the wake of a devastating earthquake and then a major cholera epidemic. I spent two deployments there, in fact, working amid scenes of terrible, heartbreaking injuries and disease. I came away from Haiti with another huge prayer burden on my heart—that God might allow me to return there to do research, that I could learn from the people of Haiti how they coped under such devastation. I could not begin to imagine how such a possibility could be brought about, I must admit. I prayed, too, that my family might be able to help a fifteen-year-old single mother have some hope of survival for herself and her child by getting her back into education in Haiti. I prayed so much about all this, though I hadn't a clue how it could happen.

As the months passed my work at home became reduced and then came a hammer blow like none other I had experienced. I was diagnosed with a critical cardiovascular problem that required urgent major surgery—a heart bypass. Having not been in hospital as a patient since I broke my leg as a teenager, and having never had any anaesthetic or surgery in my life, the prospect of such a major surgery, with all the risks the surgeons spelled out so clearly beforehand, came to me as just a tad out of normal, to say the least.

Yet, I feel I must say that it was a turning point somewhat. Of course I prayed very much, for I had no idea what this surgery would result in for me, for my family, and for my future prospects of work and an active life. It was, however, a time of immense peace as I sought to simply resign myself, my life even, into the hands and care of God. That was all I could do; it was all I wanted to do, even though so many prayers had gone unanswered for so long. I believe that peace came from God himself; knowing myself as I do I have no hesitation in affirming that. By God's grace I came through the surgery and the recovery and rehabilitation process very well. Within a few months I was invited to interview for a research post specializing in natural disasters, and I was offered the post on the basis of a proposal I constructed for research in Haiti!

Shortly after taking up this post, the husband of one of the sisters in that bereaved Taiwanese family came to the UK for the 2012 Olympic Games. He expressed a wish to visit us because he had something he needed to ask us. So, he came. He said that he had been asked by his aged father-in-law to be sure to formally invite my wife, my youngest daughter, and me to come to Taiwan because he wanted to meet us again before he died and receive us into his home. With this invitation came also our friend's invitation for me to come to his university to be a keynote speaker at a seminar, so that all our expenses would be covered as well!

Now that is not the end of the story: my friend also invited us to come to Taiwan because he and his son wanted me to baptize them, as they had now become Christians. In fact, he and his wife had been praying about this for a number of years! He added that his wife had also become a Christian and a couple of years previously she had been baptized. The reason she had been allowed to do that without causing immense offense to her father and his family, who were not Christians but espoused another religion altogether, was that he always remembered that time when a *Christian* drove all the way down to Cornwall (farther than the length of Taiwan from north to south, it seems) to help him and his family in their distress.

Thus it was that from June 2012 to February 2013 I saw the return of eight years of, at times, heart-wrenching prayer, when so often the heavens had been as brass and I cried to God, using the words of the psalmist, "How long, O Lord?!" I was able to take my wife and daughter to Taiwan to visit our friends, and I was able to return to Haiti on a major research project! What is more, throughout those years of torrid struggle in prayer, God had clearly been working behind the scenes in ways I knew absolutely nothing of at the time.

I relate this, not in any way to aggrandize myself, because for me those years were years of immense struggle, soul-searching, and heartache. I relate these things only to illustrate the mystery of God's ways at times, the mystery of providence, and also the wonderful reality of the drama of the Christian life and the roles we play, often without even being aware of it. The life of prayer is indeed an important aspect of this drama—nerve-wracking, but exciting! The story is never over until the end.

11

Prayer to a Mysterious God

SO WHAT MORE DOES THAT intriguing statement, made to the people of Israel, mean: "The secret things belong to the Lord our God, but the things that are revealed belong to us, and to our children forever, that we may do all the words of this law" (Deut 29:29)?

Well, first, God has his secrets! At first reading that may feel somewhat creepy to people living in an age when openness, disclosure, and freedom of information are enjoyed more than at any other time in living history in our democracies—yet an age, too, of conspiracy theories and distrust of government and security services. We find it hard, even odd, to associate secrecy with reverence. Secrecy tends to belong to the "dark arts."

Premoderns seemed to be able to live far more comfortably with divine mystery than we moderns. For modernists God must be reduced to our level, though many would resent considering such as being reduction. We would prefer to conceive of it as being elevation. So we invite God up to our advanced level, where human rights mean more than divine rights, and where there must be openness: no secrets. We associate secrecy with military "black ops," highly suspicious and dubious. Secrecy can also imply a cover-up of failure or even criminal conduct. It can also be a dysfunctional way of feeling important—that *you* know something significant that others do not. So, to hear that God has secrets and you will never know these because you do not need to know them can sound decidedly suspicious, especially in relation to religion—a kind of divine one-upmanship! After all, there is that category of religions that was around during the first century of the Christian church called "mystery religions." These were Gnostic pagan religions, a conglomerate of Greek and Eastern influences. They were Gnostic because they claimed to have a body of secret knowledge that only those who had been initiated, by way of some rites and experiences, could understand. Some liberal scholars have mistakenly suggested that Christianity borrowed from these more ancient mystery religions. Indeed, during the first century and, especially, the second century, forms of Gnostic thought did infiltrate the Christian church to a troublesome degree, polarizing Christians between those who had access to the secret gnosis (knowledge) and those who didn't.

In fact these two categories of gnosis are light years apart! The secrets God has can never be known—they belong to him. No amount of initiation, of incantation, of weird handshakes, of sainthood, or of praying, for that matter, will lead to their disclosure. So, unlike in the mystery religions, seeking through greater levels of devotion or service to God to gain access to these divine secrets is totally unnecessary, futile, and impossible. God has his secrets—we must live with that.

Second, there is *a sufficient revelation to make obedience to God gloriously possible.* Of the two points this is the one that is meant to take priority in our concern, and our delight. The way to keep faithful to God, to keep oneself from idolatry and every other sin, is enabled by access to what God has revealed. This is not in any way barred to our seeking and discovery—this belongs to us; it is huge and it is sufficient! As the Apostle Paul confirmed, "All Scripture is breathed out by God and profitable for teaching, for reproof, for correction, and for training in righteousness, that the man of God may be competent, equipped for every good work" (2 Tim 3:16–17). This is where all our focus is to be, then, where our concern for greater knowledge and wisdom is to concentrate, and from which the transformation of our behavior is to derive. It is, therefore, where all our praying is to be learned, and what it is to be directed by; because it is here that we come to know God best.

There is a certain amount of angst over unanswered prayer that is due to our not knowing God well enough. God is not a dispenser, nor is he a heavenly shop assistant, carefully trained to believe "the customer is always right." He is a covenant God who has graciously, and awesomely, offered to make himself known to us in a revelation that "belongs to us." Before ever we complain of unanswered prayer we should first get right on this point: we have all we could ever need to ensure we may know God as much as

Prayer to a Mysterious God

we could possibly need to, and obey him, and *trust* him, as well. I think the Apostle John had this in mind when he wrote those words regarding confidence in prayer that can puzzle us: "And this is the confidence that we have toward him, that if we ask anything *according to his will* he hears us" (1 John 5:14, emphasis mine).

Some theologians attempt to coordinate these two aspects of God—that he has secrets and that he reveals himself—by referring to the "two wills" of God: his secret will and his revealed, or permissive, will. Personally, I find that way of framing it concerning, though I understand why some think it is necessary. For me it conjures a dualism within God's being, if we are not careful, and a kind of schizoid personality—neither of which is intended and, if they were intended, would be blasphemous.[1] The two wills also can give a suspicion too easily of a divine "get-out clause" for God's not answering prayer because God always has his "other" will as an excuse! For some, this gives the impression of a "dark side," with God's "good" side being a ruse, alluring us to become victims of the other. Such Star Wars–like theological thinking cannot be justified, of course, but this does not prevent the concept worrying confused and anxious minds when prayer has gone unanswered. Professor Hans Reinders rejects the two wills idea in preference for God having one will in which "there is wisdom that is known to God alone, and there is 'a portion of wisdom prescribed for men.'" The aim of the distinction, Reinders states, is no other than to "humble our minds."[2] Therefore, even all our legitimate reading of God's will is limited and fallible. As long as we are acting within revealed boundaries of Scripture we are bidden to seek to understand the will of the Lord (Eph 5:17) and to pray accordingly, while trusting his integrity with regard to his right to exercise that portion of his wisdom that remains secret. This is appropriate knowledge of God. We do not need to know all that God knows to love and trust him as God.

The concept of God having secrets, in the sense of retaining to himself alone a portion of his wisdom, will only trouble the Christian when there is a lurking suspicion of God already. While this concept troubled Adam and Eve (Gen 3:5), it should not trouble the Christian. Adam and Eve hated being kept in the dark by God; they had to know, and the satanic promise (or,

---

1. John Piper prefers this concept of the two wills, though he states emphatically that in his view it must not imply a schizophrenia within God. Piper, "Are There Two Wills in God?" 126–27.

2. Reinders, "Providence and Ethics."

in reality, the lie) that they could know, and thus be like God, was too much to resist (Gen 3:6). The fact of Jesus Christ and the gospel must surely mean there is no ground for suspicion; in Christ we have all we need to walk in the light (1 John 1:7).

Since God is light, and in him is no darkness, and Christians walk in the light when they walk with God, there is nothing in God's secret wisdom that contradicts, or threatens our trust in, his revelation. God's secret wisdom actually serves to enhance and magnify the portion of his wisdom that is his revelation. This should, at very least, inform us that when God does answer our prayers he may do so in a way that exceeds our expectations—hence Paul could append his prayer for the Ephesian Christians with the following benediction: "Now to him who is able to do far more abundantly than all we ask or think, according to the power at work within us, to him be glory in the church and in Christ Jesus throughout all generations, forever and ever. Amen" (Eph 3:20–21). This is the focus we are meant to have, I believe. This is why, in regard to his discussion on the vexed subject of election in Rom 11, the Apostle Paul concluded that discussion of a concept profoundly connected to God's "secret things" not with a cynical rant so many of us may be prone to, but with a doxology of praise: "Oh, the depth of the riches of the wisdom and knowledge of God! How unsearchable are his judgments and how inscrutable his ways!" (Rom 11:33). It is surely right and proper that anyone who communes with God as God should accept that such an element of inscrutable mystery must coexist with the close, familiar, fellowship Scripture promises (Rom 5:5; 8:15–16; 1 John 1:3).

Thus, we come to pray, being drawn and excited to make our petitions by the revealed wisdom and promises of God and the prospect of such fellowship with God as we play our part in the drama, but also being tempered by his inscrutable mystery. That attitude will then reflect in our own spirit when we feel God is choosing not to answer our prayer: he has his reasons—reasons that are secret to us, but never against our good. The secret things that belong to God never contradict or diminish the revealed things that belong to us. There is never a cover-up, never a ruse, never a "black op." God is always light, and in him is no darkness (1 John 1:5)—not even with his secrets.

12

Omniscience and Omnipotence

AT THE ROOT OF MUCH of the anguish over unanswered prayer is a strange struggle with the ideas that God has all power and knows everything. Scholars call these ideas divine omnipotence and omniscience. It is strange (or should I say I am strange?!) because many of us will have read Ps 139 and been compelled to worship God in gratitude for the omniscience that psalm expresses. After all, is it not because we believe God knows everything that we go to him in prayer, especially when we feel we can't make sense of anything? Oh, is it not wonderful that we cannot escape from the presence of God's knowledge—even amidst the deepest clouds of shame and guilt, or at the weakest point of faith? Isn't it wonderful that even wanting to escape from God is nonsense, in view of the fact that he knows everything about us anyway? Every biological, physiological, psychological, behavioral, social, and moral thing about us is known to God. I never cease to read this psalm without amazement; do you? So, it is the very things about God that in one moment fill me with overwhelming worship from the conviction that God knows enough and is big enough to handle any crushing physical or mental health problem, any social or moral or behavioral problem, confronting me at any time. But, in the next moment, these truths can provoke me to complain, because if he knows so much and is that strong, why can he not shed light on, or do, other things I and countless others pray for so urgently? It seems that what God cannot or will not do irritates me more than what he can and will do calms me.

Hello? Is Anyone There?

This is, presumably, because I do not understand the criteria his wisdom works by, and I impart some dubious motive when that wisdom works in ways that do not please me. Those ways can seem very lottery-like: random, even unfair and callous. But, on the other hand, coming back to Ps 139, the reason that expression of divine omniscience is so wonderful is that I do not fully know myself—nor, to be honest, does anyone else, except God. At times I appear as a stranger to myself and to others, and that can be frightening to me—and to them, no doubt. Nor do I fully know the world that I inhabit. And neither do I know God in all he knows.

I think I speak for others in admitting to these limitations of understanding: at times there may be things going on within us biologically (changes, diseases, injuries, healings), psychologically (anxiety, depression, a breakdown, unspeakable joy), and spiritually (trials, spiritual depression, unanswered prayer, oppression, ecstasy). These times can be most frightening because, in all honesty, we have no idea why we are the way we are. Another psalm expresses this: "Why are you cast down, O my soul, and why are you in turmoil within me?" (Ps 42:5). Sometimes there is a reason we can identify; at other times there is none. That is how Job felt, and why so much in his speeches shows him searching, questioning, and screaming for an explanation. Isn't it interesting, and instructive, that the only answer he got that worked for him was that of God's omniscience and omnipotence (Job 38–41)?

Is it not a delightful relief for the Christian that she can come before God in prayer and reveal all—however rotten or sordid, cruel or humiliating? However heartbreaking or shameful the issue may be in one's life, there is this blessed Person you can speak to; he knows about it anyway, and he cares because he always hears. Do not despise the ministry of God's presence for you! He is unshockable, and we shall never take him by surprise.

In my work in trauma care I learned a long time ago that the most significant contribution a trauma responder can make in the early stages often has nothing to do with what you say, or the dynamic agenda you bring with you, or the astute theology you feel has equipped you to supply answers. It's more about the fact that you just took the time to show up there *for them*, for the sufferers. When I was deployed to Haiti in the wake of the terrible earthquake that devastated that already shattered country in 2010, I worked in the cholera treatment centers, among Haitians who were now retraumatized by cholera; so many of those dear people found hope just because God had brought us all the way from the UK to be there, to

Omniscience and Omnipotence

pray with them and hold them in their weakness. In the throes of trauma we often don't need or want someone to *talk* to us, to give us their views on why it happened or how we should cope. That is not the answer we most need then. Our shattered minds can't cope with the why and the how so early on. But we are so thankful when someone is just there because they care and know how not to say a word—a blessed art! So, why do we so quickly despise God when he does just that—when, in response to our pain and heartbreak, to our moaning, ranting and raging, he comes in silence and is there with us? We see this principle in the way God responded to the anger and depression of Elijah:

> And behold the LORD passed by, and a great and strong wind tore the mountains and broke in pieces the rocks before the LORD, but the LORD was not in the wind. And after the wind an earthquake. But the LORD was not in the earthquake. And after the earthquake a fire, but the LORD was not in the fire. And after the fire the sound of a low whisper [margin: *a thin silence*]. (1 Kgs 19:11–12)

Sometimes there are answers, and God has them, but we are not in any shape to hear or absorb them yet. Psalm 139, I find, provides this divine ministry of presence, of a thin silence—I think that is why the psalmist wrote it.

Jonathan Edwards, the great American philosopher-theologian and pastor of the eighteenth century, often reflected on prayer, including unanswered prayer, and God's omniscience and omnipotence figured highly in those reflections. Edwards considered omniscience a wonderful attribute of God for the pray-er, since it guaranteed nothing could be overlooked in regard to any prayer request, because God knows all things from the beginning. So, we can take comfort in Jesus' teaching not to "heap up empty phrases"—not to go on and on in prayer so as to be heard—because "your Father knows what you need before you ask him" (Matt 6:7–8). Now some of us, when in a down and cynical mood, might ask, "Well, if God knows what I want before I ask him, then why do I need to ask him at all?!" Edwards, however, preferred to take Jesus' words of divine sovereignty as sheer encouragement rather than annoyance. In a sense, the choice between the two lies with us. We can choose to believe God's omniscience makes prayer into annoying nonsense, or we can choose to believe his omniscience ensures that prayer is immensely effective. Divine omniscience mocks prayer, or it complements prayer; that is the choice we have. Furthermore, omniscience assures us that God knows what is best for us; he works according to his own plan and timing. Omniscience provides a solid base to our need for patience and waiting, therefore.

God's omnipotence becomes important particularly at times when the answers to our prayers are long delayed or just seem bizarre and confusing. We have two prayers in Scripture in which divine omnipotence has played a key role in giving comfort during such times. The first concerns the Old Testament prophet Jeremiah at a most depressing and distressing point in his life. The event is recorded for us in Jer 32. In those days the city of Jerusalem—God's city, as it were—was undergoing a cruel, merciless siege by Nebuchadnezzar's Babylonian army. Conditions inside the city were absolutely appalling, with famine, sickness, and dreadful suffering, all of which the prophet was witnessing and struggling over within himself. It was the lowest point in the history of God's covenant people. Their defeat and exile were imminent! The pressure upon Jeremiah too was relentless. Not only did he have to experience the horrors and discomforts of the siege himself, he had to serve God by continuing to preach God's ministry of judgment upon Judah and the inevitable exile; and he had to suffer threats to his life from Judah's king, Zedekiah, who much preferred the unreality of believing Jerusalem's inhabitants "never, never, never will be slaves."

While in the midst of this crisis, Jeremiah was asked by God to purchase a plot of land, which was offered to him by his cousin, and for which Jeremiah possessed "the right of redemption for purchase" (Jer 32:7). The whole procedure was attended to with watertight legal detail. Then Jeremiah instructed his scribe, Baruch, to place the title deed in an earthenware pot, to ensure the deeds would last for a long time, ready for burial under the field. Jeremiah then prayed a most moving and—to many of us who are troubled by unanswered prayer—humbling prayer:

> Ah, Lord God! It is you who have made the heavens and the earth by your great power, and by your outstretched arm! Nothing is too hard for you. You show steadfast love to thousands, but you repay the guilt of fathers to their children after them, O great and mighty God whose name is the Lord of Hosts great in counsel and mighty in deed, whose eyes are open to all the ways of the children of man, rewarding each one according to his ways and according to the fruit of his deeds. You have shown signs and wonders in the land of Egypt, and to this day in Israel and among all mankind, and have made a name for yourself as at this day. You brought your people Israel out of the land of Egypt with signs and wonders, with a strong hand and outstretched arm, and with great terror. And

you gave them this land, which you swore to their fathers to give them, a land flowing with milk and honey. And they entered and took possession of it. But they did not obey your voice or walk in your law. They did nothing of all you commanded them to do. Therefore you have made all this disaster come upon them. Behold the siege mounds have come up to the city to take it, and because of sword and famine and pestilence the city is given into the hands of the Chaldeans who are fighting against it. What you spoke has come to pass, and behold, you see it. Yet you, O Lord God, have said to me, "Buy this field for money and get witnesses"—though the city is given into the hands of the Chaldeans. (Jer 32:17–25)

In that prayer Jeremiah reflected upon the way God had delivered Israel by the exodus from Egypt and brought them into the promised land. Yet, Israel had not obeyed God and had brought this disastrous judgment upon itself. Jeremiah could see that exile was now inevitable. The unthinkable and unimaginable was surely to happen, despite so much praying that it wouldn't! Right at the end of his prayer, however, he says, "Yet you, O Lord God, have said to me, 'Buy the field for money and get witnesses'—though the city is given into the hands of the Chaldeans" (v. 25). By instructing the prophet to purchase the field, the Lord was indicating that people would return again to that place in due course. Now, what helped Jeremiah believe this was a promise God would not renege on, even though from the current perspective it seemed hopeless. It was his conviction of God as omnipotent. For at the very beginning of his prayer, he says, "Nothing is too hard for you" (v. 17)—a truth that was confirmed by God himself in his immediate answer to Jeremiah's prayer: "Behold, I am the Lord, the God of all flesh. Is there anything too hard for me?" (v. 27).

Now, Jeremiah could have used his belief in God's omnipotence to think, "Well, because nothing is too hard for you, Lord, you can answer my prayer right now for this siege and exile, with all the suffering and loss of life, to stop." Instead, realizing the justice of what was being allowed to happen, he trusted in God's omnipotence for an encouraging outcome, in God's appointed time. Belief in God's omnipotence is meant as a comfort to be enjoyed as we wait for the outcome of our prayers, not as a problem to torment us during that wait. The Apostle James reminds us, "As an example of suffering and patience, brothers, take the prophets who spoke in the name of the Lord" (Jas 5:10). Jeremiah was one such prophet worth taking note of in contending with unanswered prayer.

Hello? Is Anyone There?

The second example comes in the New Testament, with the announcement of the birth of the Messiah to Mary, which is recorded in Luke 1:28–38. The angel Gabriel explains to Mary how the Son of God will be conceived in her womb, not by union with Joseph, her espoused husband, but by the Holy Spirit prior to her marriage to Joseph. Mary's response, understandably, was, "How will this be, since I am a virgin?" (v. 34). Some further explanation is given that ends with the words, "For nothing is impossible with God" (v. 35), to which truth Mary's response was, "Behold I am the servant of the Lord, let it be to me according to your word." In other words, don't demand that God's omnipotence or omniscience, his power or knowledge, be proven to you by his having to dot every *i* and cross every *t* in relation to what he says about your situation; just trust him, because of his omnipotence and his omniscience. Let these be your comfort and encouragement during times of confusion in which belief and unbelief vie with one another because the outcome is unclear.

Jonathan Edwards was positive in his belief in these attributes of God in regard to prayer, even though he was not unsympathetic to those who struggled with unanswered prayers. He believed that God sometimes delays his answers so that all will serve to his glory and not our own, so that we learn first to acknowledge his goodness and our dependence upon God in this; and in so doing, our wills will become molded to his—thus ensuring the grounds for answered prayer![1]

Again, God's omnipotence was never seen as a need to leave off praying because God will only do what we ask if he chooses, not because we ask him. On the contrary, an essential aspect of the doctrine of divine omnipotence is the parallel truth of God decreeing he will do his will through the prayers of his people. In fact, it is in the balanced way that Scripture narratives both acknowledge divine omniscience and omnipotence *and* describe the way people prayed, that we can best come to terms with the enigmas that seem apparent. I will not attempt to resolve those enigmas by philosophizing some rationale that will lay them to rest in our heads. That would require entering forbidden territory, namely into the divine decrees, into the "secret things." In my view, Peter Greig's otherwise helpful book *God on Mute* falls down at the point he begins to attempt such a resolution for the doctrines of divine sovereignty and human responsibility, a resolution

---

1. The American scholar Peter Beck has researched Edwards' works extensively, and I acknowledge my indebtedness to him for many of my comments on Edwards' theology of prayer. See Beck, *The Voice of Faith*; he addresses the issue of unanswered prayer especially in pages 40–54.

he continues to appeal to periodically thereafter in the book. He becomes jammed between the doors of his view of human free will and the fallenness of human nature. It is disappointing that, at this point, he seems to draw more upon the philosophical focus of some contemporary scholars on the "mystery of human freedom" than on the scriptural acknowledgment of the mystery of God's sovereignty.[2] By far our safest approach is to accept both human freedom and divine sovereignty in the compatible manner in which they are narrated in the biblical drama.

In fact, the biblical drama reveals a complex of emotions in God that would require us to be God to understand. Given that prospect is justly beyond us, we have to come to terms with living with this complexity. Pastor and writer John Piper expresses the issue as follows:

> God's emotional life is infinitely complex beyond our ability to fully comprehend. For example, who can comprehend that the Lord hears in one moment of time the prayers of ten million Christians around the world, and sympathizes with each one personally and individually like a caring Father (as Hebrews 4:15 says he will), even though among those ten million prayers some are brokenhearted and some are bursting with joy? How can God weep with those who weep and rejoice with those who rejoice when they are both coming to him at the same time—in fact are always coming to him with no break at all?[3]

We might add the thought, "With similar emotions God can reveal himself as a prayer-hearing God and also choose, for reasons his higher perspective sees best, to delay, or answer differently, some of those prayers from the brokenhearted." God's omniscience and omnipotence give him the ability to make such decisions, confusing to us, but in a manner that is safe for us.

---

2. For instance, see Pinnock, *Grace of God*, 25–26.
3. Piper, "Are There Two Wills in God?" 126–27.

13

Knowing the Answerer

ONE APPROACH TO HELPING WITH the mystery of God's sovereignty in prayer has been to go back to a particular aspect of providence. In regard to prayer there are three questions that come up: Does God *hear* my prayer? Does he *want* to respond to it? Has he the *ability* to respond? The scriptural doctrine of God as omnipotent, as Jonathan Edwards rightly argued, responds to all three questions with a resounding "*Yes!*" But therein lies the problem, especially for prayers made in regard to evil and suffering—and so many of our anguished prayers are made with reference to one or both of these.

Since God is light and in him is no darkness at all (1 John 1:5), and he is "of purer eyes than to see evil and cannot look at wrong" (Hab 1:13), then it seems nothing could be more certain to gain his interest than prayers that beg him to curtail some evil—whether it be the safe recovery of a hostage from a terrorist act, or the deliverance of a young child from a habitual molester, or the end of a genocidal war, or the healing of a gifted Christian so she can better serve the interests of the kingdom of God. In fact, the list is endless. So, divine silence to such prayers is confusing and discouraging if God does hear prayer and yet is willing and able to answer. It was so for Habakkuk, which is why he struggled to make any sense out of God's allowing the predatory and cruel Chaldeans, whose god was their might, to overrun God's own people (Hab 1:12–17). Similar confusion and hurt surfaces also in regard to suffering, which is why Jesus sweat drops of blood as he pleaded with God in Gethsemane in the shadow of the way of the cross (Luke 22:41–44), but got only silence in return.

Habitually, some Christians have resorted to something called theodicy to try to make some sense of evil and suffering and the apparent failure of prayer to penetrate the armor of these problems. Theodicy is the attempt to justify God, to provide a kind of rationale for what he does that also makes sense to us humans. Does it work? Does it calm the troubled breast? Clearly not, otherwise many of us who have dipped our toe into the "healing pool" of theodicy would not still have the problems we do. Having said that, it really all depends on what kind of approach you take.

Basically, there are two approaches of theodicy: philosophical and practical. Some brief reflection on these might be helpful at this point.

Philosophical Theodicy

To be honest, much contemporary theological and philosophical scholarship and pastoral care sees little benefit from philosophical theodicy: that is, the attempt to produce a philosophical rationale that justifies God's acting as he does. While this may draw upon Scripture, the adjudicating factor will, in the end, be human reason. It is based on the modernist belief that there is a universal realm of reason that is able to adjudicate on everything, even religion—a belief that is being increasingly discounted by a postmodernism that holds that everyone can adjudicate for, and on, herself alone. However, the Bible reveals God working according to a different wisdom (1 Cor 1:20–31). This is a wisdom that promotes the glory of God's grace rather than our supreme right to know all. Therefore, from a Christian perspective there is no rational reason why God, in whom we believe for the salvation of our souls, should require justifying. And what authority does unaided human reason (personal or universal) possess to attempt such a work anyway?

Surely Abraham got it spot on when he, in the context of his intercessory prayer for his nephew, Lot, said, "Shall not the judge of all the earth do what is just?" (Gen 18:25). Yet, these words were uttered in the context of Abraham's pleading with God over the sparing of his nephew. God's wisdom allows for both trusting in the Lord to do the right, just thing and reasoning with him from the perspective of our own brokenheartedness.

Reflecting on the 2004 Indian Ocean earthquake and tsunami, Orthodox scholar David Bentley Hart maintains that it is a hopeless agenda to pursue a theodicy for a "total explanation." He judges, "The New Testament also teaches us that . . . suffering and death—considered in themselves—have no true meaning or purpose at all; and this is in a very real sense the most liberating and joyous wisdom that the gospel imparts."[1] Kenneth Surin considers theodicy to be inherently flawed, because "it requires us to be articulate, rational and reasonable in the face of that which is so often unspeakable," and he concludes,

> Theodicy, it could be said, is always doomed to be at variance with the profound truth that the "problem of evil" will cease to be such only when evil and suffering no longer exist on this earth. Until that time there is much substance in the charge that the theodicist's presumption . . . only trivializes the pain and suffering of those who are victims. It is therefore necessary to stress that we are not likely to bring much comfort to the victims of suffering with a theodicy.[2]

Trivializing something that can cause so much pain is not an option for the Christian sufferer or carer, nor is it their role to take the place of God in justifying God. Furthermore, theodicy can be a real impediment to healing because it focuses upon a painful event and keeps it in the memory unjustifiably, and provokes continuing anguish of spirit.

In short, I believe philosophical theodicy is in fact incompatible with Christianity because it doesn't view life through the lens of Christ and the cross. It also represents a flight from reality into theoretical philosophic speculation that creates more problems than it solves. The late John Stott rightly concluded,

> It needs to be said at once that the Bible supplies no thorough solution to the problem of evil, whether "natural" evil or "moral." . . . Its purpose is more practical than philosophical. Consequently, although there are references to sin and suffering on virtually every page, its concern is not to explain their origin but to help us to overcome them.[3]

Philosophical theodicy is a creature of Enlightenment arrogance, which has been encouraged into existence by the failure of a robust revelation-based Christianity. In premodern times there was an almost universal acceptance

---

1. Hart, *Doors of the Sea*, 35.
2. Surin, "Problem of Evil," 198.
3. Stott, *Cross of Christ*, 312.

of some form of biblical providence doctrine. Few sought comfort in theodicy then, and I am not convinced those who seek it there now will find significant answers to unanswered prayer. In the words of P. T. Forsyth: intellectually naive though it may seem to modernity, Christianity "is not the sacrifice we make, but the sacrifice we trust; not the victory we win, but the victory we inherit. That is the evangelical principle. We do not see the answer; but we trust the Answerer, and measure by Him."[4]

If theodicy is to help, then it must help with trusting the Answerer, even when he doesn't answer or we don't understand the answer! Knowing the Answerer is the key rather than knowing the answers.

Practical Theodicy—the Gospel

The word from the Answerer is found in Christ and his cross and resurrection. I agree with Forsyth, therefore, that Christ is God's revealed theodicy of grace: "It is not a rational triumph but a victory of faith. Christ is the theodicy of God and the justifier both of God and the ungodly. The supreme theodicy is atonement."[5] Forsyth wrote these words in a book reflecting upon the horrors of the First World War, a time when so many prayers were made, and so many seemed to go unanswered. What he says seems very close to the affirmation of the Apostle Paul, when he stated of the cross-work of Christ, "It was to show his righteousness at the present time, so that he might be just and the justifier of the one who has faith in Jesus" (Rom 3:26). This statement was Paul's pastoral response for the benefit of Christians, praying for the awful persecution and suffering they were enduring to cease, but during which, even so, many Christians would lose their work or even their lives.

However, some postmodern scholars suggest such a traditional fall/redemption motif holds a devastating psychological corollary because it is built upon fear and not the psychologies of trust. Any kind of psychological care built upon fear is invalid, they argue. Now, I would not dispute that trust is essential to Christianity and to prayer, and trust can be abused in the interests of someone using fear for quick fixes or to build religious empires. I believe some televangelists and healers engage in such abuse when they subtly play on the fears of seriously sick people and their families, promising healing in return for a financial donation.

4. Forsyth, *Justification of God*, 230.
5. Ibid., 175.

Hello? Is Anyone There?

As one who believes the traditional motif is mistaken, Matthew Fox starts with the assumption that God first needs to earn our trust by doing a lot more in our favor—and presumably must, therefore, answer our prayers as a way of so earning our trust. However, I dispute the assumption that the fall/redemption motif does not teach trust. In the biblical drama, human sin has caused a huge barrier in relating to God and has brought expulsion, punishment, and alienation upon humans. We are, at the end of the day, always more guilty and deserving of wrath than wounded and deserving of pity. In this state (and its effects upon creation as a whole) a due amount of fear is perfectly apposite.[6] It is, therefore, more to the point to say that God cannot trust us, and we dare not trust ourselves! Therefore, only under God's covenant terms of redemption can trust become viable, because God's covenant is built upon his faithfulness, not ours. Trust (faith) is the key component called for to secure the justification that flows from the redemptive work of God's grace. In the redemptive work on the cross and in the resurrection God has demonstrated he is most surely trustworthy. This is what he has done in response to the evil and suffering about which so much prayer is made.

In summary: it is the drama of fall, divine redemption and reconciliation that is the answer to the struggles of unanswered prayer. We put this question to God: "What have you done, that we can trust you in the silence?" And we are given a resounding answer: "This is my beloved Son, hear him!"[7]

In respect of Christ as our Savior, God cannot ever be accused of silence, other than the silence of his presence I referred to earlier. The gospel is not silence, it is proclamation—in the Greek, it is *euangelion* and *kerygma*, good news and proclamation in the sense of international headlines, to use the media vocabulary of today. And, ironically, this redemption and reconciliation have also been achieved via the pathway of the unanswered prayer of our Savior. Bearing our sin and drawing upon himself the requisite judgment of God such sin deserves, he cried in anguish from the cross, "My God, my God, why have you forsaken me?" and got no answer. That silence was a necessity for the redemption Christ was providing.

So, let no one say unanswered prayer has no use, or that all is lost or without meaning if our prayers are not answered. Humanity's greatest need was secured by a mysterious providence. It was secured in the context of

---

6. According to Gen 3:10, "I heard Your voice in the garden, and I was afraid . . ."
7. Mark 9:7. See also Mark 12:1–11.

a most anguished unanswered prayer, where a divine-human being, with real human nature, surrendered himself to the most appalling prospect any being could contemplate, on the basis of simply trusting God: "Yet not my will, but what you will" (Mark 14:36). Back in the shadows of the Old Testament, it was some awareness of this practical concept of God's omnipotence that enabled Job, during one of his "lightbulb moments," to say, "Though he slay me, I will hope in him" (Job 13:15). Indeed, in the end it was what God has done in divine omnipotence, not any philosophic discourse on evil and suffering, that brought Job to his knees in worship and trust: "*I know that you can do all things*, and that no purpose of yours can be thwarted" (Job 42:2, emphasis mine).

So, there ought not to be any disquiet in our relationship with God's omniscience and omnipotence, only love and trust. The problem with the more philosophical kind of theodicy is that it tends to assume we have a human right to a fair and just life, one in which everything ought to work to produce our happiness, both through events turning out well and understanding being given to us. We struggle with the fact that we don't deserve any of what this assumption promises! We struggle with the bottom line, which is that life is a big mess, that's just the way it is, and we have a hand in continuing this mess every day. If we can get over that struggle and really trust things as God reveals, then we might have the perspective Peter Greig puts into words when he says, "It will be our blessings more than our sufferings that provoke us to ask God, 'Why?'"[8]

That I am writing this book is indicative that for many of us the problem still lies in a skewed vision of the way the world really is and of who God is; that is why we ask "Why?" so often. Only because of divine omniscience and omnipotence can the vision be different. As Peter Beck has stated, "In true prayer—prayer that pleases God—man admits that God is God and he is not."[9] When prayers seem unanswered, don't hate the twins of omniscience and omnipotence, love God for them!

When I began writing this book, a line from a well-known hymn kept buzzing through my mind: "What a friend we have in Jesus." You may know the hymn, and how it goes on to encourage us that whatever the problem—sin, grief, trials, temptations, forsakenness, weakness, burden—we should "take it to the Lord in prayer." To be honest, I have found that hymn hard to sing when it seems that urgent, heartbroken prayers made to God through

---

8. Greig, *God On Mute*, 123.
9. Beck, *Voice of Faith*, 37.

Jesus have not been answered. In those moments I have not felt Jesus to be a very good friend. How do you cope with feeling your best friend has dumped you when you most need him? Well, having some idea about how that hymn came to be where it is today in the Christian ranks of spiritual song may help; it will certainly be sobering, as it was to me.

Joseph Scriven was a new Dublin graduate of twenty-five years old, engaged to be married to the love of his life. The day before his wedding day his fiancée was thrown from her horse into a river as she crossed a bridge on the way to meet him. Joseph tried in vain to save her but she drowned. Heartbroken, he emigrated to Canada to be a teacher. Some twelve years or so later he fell in love again, with Eliza Stokes. However, before his new wedding day could happen Eliza fell ill and died. Joseph's mother, back in Ireland, was heartbroken for her shattered son, and she too became very ill. Joseph could not visit her, so he wrote her a poem and sent it to her, to encourage her. That poem became the hymn, and the rest is history.

In his book *Creation Untamed: The Bible, God, and Natural Disasters*, Old Testament scholar Terence Fretheim intriguingly has a reflection on the significance of prayer to the way we react to natural disasters. Of course, times and circumstances of grievous tragedy and trauma are notorious for raising the problem of unanswered prayer, so he is right to reflect on this in the context of natural disasters.

Fretheim argues that the images of God we construct have a significant bearing on our attitude to prayer and can, in fact, skew our view of God and make us deaf to what the texts may actually be saying. In the place of such "extreme images of God" he argues that the root image in regard to God and prayer should be that of relatedness. Prayer is just an aspect of the relationship a Christian has with God.[10] That relationship, however, is bigger than the prayer aspect, though the relationship has an influence on prayer. Therefore he suggests that rather than looking for or expecting "answers" to prayer, we ought to think in terms of "responses." A focus on answers tends to narrow our expectation: "The word 'answers' often carries such a level of specificity that the pray-ers' horizons are sharply limited, and they often look for efficacy in the wrong places."[11] This, he concludes, then limits our expectation of an answer to being either a categorical "yes" or "no." A true, healthy relationship will not make such demands, nor will it offer such categorical answers to all requests. In a healthy relationship between

---

10. Fretheim, *Creation Untamed*, 131–35.
11. Ibid., 137.

the Christian and God there must be the aspect of the non-categorical, the "maybe/maybe not," which leaves the Christian with the issue hanging, unresolved, but always in the context of a good relationship with God.

Trusting the Answerer *is* the answer for no answers!

14

Privileged for Accessible Grace

IN A BOOK THAT DELIBERATELY focuses on the *problem* of unanswered prayer it would be remiss to neglect the enormous attention given in Scripture to the positive encouragements to pray and to answered prayer—the *privilege* of prayer. Such neglect could give the impression that it is my contention that the problem of unanswered prayer makes the actual act of praying a nonsense, which is the furthest thing from my intention. The purpose has been to acknowledge the problem, to examine it realistically, and to respond to it constructively so that praying becomes even more attractive and effective, not less. Prayer becomes a privilege worth struggling with, in other words.

In this focus on the positive encouragements to pray I could refer again to those texts mentioned in chapter 1, which confirm how strong the emphasis is within Scripture on God as a prayer-answering God. I hope it is becoming increasingly clear that while my aim has been to meet the problem head-on, not to ignore it, in the end a resolution boils down to a matter of theological perspective, not to anecdotal evidence. For every anecdotal account of unanswered prayer there are many more for answered prayers, and the actual theology of encouragement to pray far exceeds any focus on the problems as far as Scripture is concerned. I have no business minimizing the problems, just as Scripture doesn't do so, as I have attempted to show; but I do believe the problems do not overwhelm the privilege of prayer. Thus, we may choose to focus on the problems if we wish, but that would be like concentrating on a speck of soot on a masterpiece, rather than standing back and admiring the real scene or portrait to such an extent you can hardly see the speck. On God's masterpiece, however, there is no real speck, just occasional strange shades we cannot yet understand.

One of the most beautiful and moving parts of the biblical drama (or masterpiece, to retain the above metaphor for the moment) is the account of the life of Abraham and his wife, Sarah. Their struggle with God in regard to prayer is profoundly moving. It also brings together the aspects of grace and trust that are crucial to our reducing the problem of unanswered prayer. Two parts to this narrative spring to mind: the promise of a son, and the call to sacrifice the son. The first represents the major scene in the masterpiece, the second a strange shade that is not easy to understand.

The Promise of a Son

God gave Abraham and Sarah a huge promise: he would make of them a great nation; God would mightily bless them and, through them, bless all the families of the earth. "Now the LORD said to Abram, 'Go from your country and your kindred and your father's house to the land that I will show you. And I will make of you a great nation, and I will bless you and make your name great, so that you will be a blessing. I will bless those who bless you, and him who dishonors you I will curse, and in you all the families of the earth shall be blessed" (Gen 12:1–3). That meant having at least one male child, therefore. But it is stated from the very outset of the narrative that Sarah was biologically incapable of bearing children (Gen 11:30). It seems that understanding that fact from the outset was essential to the drama that was to unfold. To begin with, Abraham and Sarah seemed to handle this prospect quite well, apart from a hiccup in Egypt when, to save his own life, Abraham passed Sarah off as his sister. As the years rolled on it seemed hard for them to discern any development of the promise—about which it is impossible to imagine Abraham and Sarah never praying, individually and together. Yet, by the time God renewed the promise by telling Abraham, "Fear not, Abram, I am your shield; your reward shall be very great" (Gen 15:1), clearly doubts had set in. Abraham shared these in his prayers: "O Lord GOD, what shall you give me, for I continue childless. . . . Behold, you have given me no offspring" (15:2–3). Again some further assurance was given to them by God: "Look toward heaven, and number the stars, if you are able to number them. . . . So shall your offspring be" (15:5). But what sort of an answer must that have seemed if the all-important prayer was never answered—"Please, can we have a child?" So the drama goes on: year after year passes by, and still no child. Sarah has all but given up on God's promise and their prayer ever being answered, which is why she hatched the plan for her slave, Hagar, to become a surrogate mom (Gen 16:1–6). This indicates Abraham had given up, too, since he went ahead with the botched affair and its painful sequel. This is unanswered praying with a hurtful vengeance!

Next, we are told Abraham has reached ninety-nine years of age, and Sarah ninety, when yet another promise comes from God (Gen 17:1–2). Whereas the New Testament writer to the Hebrews puts it very modestly of Sarah, "even when she was past the age" (Heb 11:11), the comment on Abraham is very blunt: "and him as good as dead" (Heb 11:12)! So, still no child, and no prospect of having one. In fact, at this stage of there being no answer, no child, Sarah doesn't know whether to laugh or cry whenever the issue is raised, so she laughs to herself at the absurdity of their producing progeny (Gen 18:12). What commenced as a divine promise for this dear woman—that the worst thing that could happen to her, her being incapable of bearing children, would be transformed so she could bear a son for Abraham—turned into years and years of nothing but seemingly empty promises and unanswered prayers, dashing every hope inside her.

However, at the appointed time (Gen 18:14), God's time, the answer came and it was glorious; God was as good as his word (18:13–14; 21:1). Yet the better part of Sarah's life had passed by in waiting.

You see, there is potential for immense frustration and heartbreak if we insist on defining "answer" in the way we did at the beginning: "within the petitioner's expectations." God does not work by our calendar or according to our expectations. Why should he? It is his glory that is at stake, not our pleasure. I know that is not an easy principle for human nature to accept. But it is precisely because God can work to his own time, and to his own expectations, that life under God's reign, with its appointed times, is so full of glorious surprises, of things working out that are beyond our expectations (Eph 3:20). He has his own "appointed time." That is the reason the Old Testament church prayed for hundreds of years without an answer—until the "fullness of the time" (Gal 4:4), at which time came the Messiah who was beyond everyone's expectations. Similarly, throughout the long, unanswered, prayerful vigils of Simeon and Anna the same principle was working (Luke 2:22–38). Think of it: *by our definition*, we are where we are today, as Christians in this wonderful drama of grace, where we can speak with God as friend and father whenever we wish, on the basis of a seemingly unanswered prayer! We possess an access no one can take away from us even if they wanted to strip us of every privilege we have!

The Sacrifice of the Son

But there is more from Abraham as a test case. Next, after all those years he has his son, Isaac—the *son of God's promise*, don't forget—but also a son who increasingly *gripped Abraham's heart*. He was special in so many ways, as God reminded Abraham just at the time he instructed him to kill Isaac! God seemed to metaphorically stab the knife into Abraham immediately prior to Abraham's being expected to literally stab the knife into Isaac. For God said, "Take your *son*, your *only* son Isaac, whom *you love*, and go to the land of Moriah, and offer him there as a burnt offering on one of the mountains of which I shall tell you" (Gen 22:2, emphasis mine). In our age of child protection, and the rights of the child, such a request sounds monstrously offensive—a thing you would account as unthinkable of a righteous God, unless God himself made it clear he actually did request it. But, even then, why should a God who, in the outplaying of the Old Testament drama, so condemned child sacrifice, here sanction it for his own purposes? Imagine how Abraham must have felt—how he must have prayed! Did God think Abraham was made of stone, to ask such a thing of him? But, in fact, Abraham chose not to countenance the thoughts of a merciless God; he chose to trust and obey instead.

Remember what we said earlier, with regard to Moses leading the Israelites at the Red Sea? Prayer is not a substitute for obedience. In fact, not until Abraham had obeyed did he get any answer to any questions going round in his head concerning the purpose of sacrificing Isaac—his son, his only son, the son whom he loved! The author of the Letter to the Hebrews interprets that Abraham coped with this by an act of faith. He did not question the morality of God's command to sacrifice Isaac. He did choose to believe that even if his obedience to God did, for some reason, end in the death of Isaac, "of whom it was said, 'Through Isaac shall your offspring be named,'" then "he considered that God was able even to raise him from the dead" (Heb 11:18, 19).

What these two Abrahamic scenarios combine to teach us is this: prayer, trust, and grace operate together in a symphony for prayer to be effective. What is more, they operate in different measures, according to different circumstances. Sometimes, when we pray we just have to throw ourselves into God's arms of grace and trust him for what seems like ages, and against what can seem absurd odds. "No answer" must not be taken to mean "No," but it can mean "Not yet; wait—a long wait, maybe an unresolved wait." Yet, without a firm relationship with God in terms of his grace, it will be hard to cope because it will be hard to trust. The problem of unanswered prayer can assume such large proportions that it blots out the dramatic masterpiece and the beauty of prayer.

My concern in this chapter, therefore, is to encourage us to gaze, worshipfully, on the real masterpiece of God and prayer. For the Christian, gazing upon God, getting the right perspective on the divine masterpiece, can only be achieved by observing from the angle of grace. Any other perspective, more likely than not, will give us a skewed view, which may well draw our focus back to the problems again.

I am persuaded that, as with so many of our problems with aspects of the Christian faith, the issues with unanswered prayer have little to do with discipline or technique or poor methods, though these may have their place, but are almost entirely consequences of a dysfunctional view of God's grace. Therefore, the best way of helping address the problem of unanswered prayer is good theology, a correct view of God. Since prayer is all about the act of approaching and communicating with God, then our view of the God we think we are approaching will be hugely significant in the problems we judge to be present and in the manner we are able to resolve those problems.

So, what perspective do the Scriptures present us of God in regard to prayer, as viewed from a theology of grace?

An immediate statement that springs to mind is found in the Old Testament prophecy of Isa 55:8–9: "For my thoughts are not your thoughts, neither are your ways my ways, declares the LORD. For as the heavens are higher than the earth, so my ways are higher than your ways and my thoughts than your thoughts." This remarkable statement of grace is of interest for at least two reasons: first, because it draws together the attributes of divine omniscience and mystery. God has knowledge, he has thoughts and ways. But these are not on the same level of understanding as ours are; they are different. That should be no surprise. It is appropriate that we cannot always understand all of God's thoughts and ways. But that fact does not make those thoughts and ways unfair, bad, or cruel, or at all suspicious. They are just different; they stem from a different, "secret" portion of God's wisdom. However, they are the thoughts and ways that always respond to our prayers, operating on a higher plane than the best of ours.

A second reason these words are of interest is they are also an explanation of the constitution of grace. We know that because they follow on immediately from an equally incredible invitation of grace in the previous two verses: "Seek the LORD while he may be found; call upon him while he is near; let the wicked forsake his own way, and the unrighteous man his thoughts; let him return to the LORD, that he may abundantly pardon." Words from God to sinful humans don't come much more graciously than that! Left to our thoughts we could never return to the Lord and find abundant pardon. We just would not want to, or if we did, we would not believe that God would welcome us. So, these words represent the ultimate gracious invitation!

Put these two reasons together and we conclude: if God has his secrets, his own appointed times, these never cease to operate in the interests of God's priority of grace.

Another resort to the theology of Jonathan Edwards can help us get this perspective right. My only departure from Edwards, I think, is that whereas he views the priority arising out of the divine attributes being God's own glory, I believe it is God's love—that God is glorified most in his grace. However, the difference is a moot one.

For my current purposes I focus on a single sermon Edwards preached to his Northampton congregation, dated January 8th, 1735–36.[1] It is a significant sermon because it was preached to a congregation that was living in fear of a life-threatening epidemic that had hit part of the city of Boston, Massachusetts, not far from Northampton. Having myself been present, back in 2010–11, in the Caribbean country of Haiti during the peak of a cholera epidemic, which killed over seven thousand people and severely infected many thousands more, I can get a feel of the kind of fear an epidemic can create. Such fear also provokes people to a lot of prayer! Issues of chronic health are probably the most prayed over and the most difficult to come to terms with when seemingly unanswered: praying believers can die while non-praying unbelievers can live. In Haiti, not everyone's prayers for cholera patients were answered—including mine! I recall a young man being carried to the cholera treatment center on a motorbike. He had come down from a village in the mountains with his mother. Once he had been admitted we got to talking and I prayed with him and his mother. Often

---

1. Edwards, "Most High a Prayer-Hearing God," 113–18.

during that day I would wave to him and him back to me with a smile. The next day he took ill with suspected meningitis, and in the evening, as I went off duty, I took my leave of him and his mother. A couple of days later I returned to duty at the center and looked out for him and his mother. They were nowhere to be seen. I made inquiry after them and was informed he had died and the mother had returned home. I felt really gutted by this news, for I had prayed so hard for them both. I knew how much that mother loved her son, and how worried she was for him.

No doubt this was the same in Edwards's day in Northampton, as people were wondering if God would hear their prayers and spare them or their loved ones, and how they would cope if he didn't. Edwards's pastoral response included preaching a sermon titled "The Most High a Prayer-Hearing God." It was based on the psalmist's worshipful affirmation at the opening of Ps 65: "O Thou that hearest prayer" (v. 2, Authorized Version). In the typical Puritan manner of preaching, Edwards drew a single doctrinal point out of the text for exposition and application. This point was: "That it is the character of the Most High, that he is a God who hears prayer." In his second main point in that sermon, in order to prove God is *eminently* a God who hears prayer, Edwards focused upon aspects of God's grace. A summary of the points he made will make an excellent contemporary focus for us as we struggle with the short-sightedness over things we can't see and pass over the beauty of what we can see.

First, Edwards refers to the *free access* we have been granted to God in prayer. The throne of grace is open for us to come boldly to God (Heb 4:14, 16), whatsoever kind of person we may be (1 Cor 1:2, 3). He says, "Yea, God allows the most vile and unworthy; the greatest of sinners are allowed to come through Christ. And he not only allows, but encourages, and frequently invites them; yea manifests himself as delighting in being sought to by prayer."

Second, God hears us *readily*. Even when he chooses to delay communicating his answer to us he still takes notice the moment we pray, as was the case with Daniel's delayed answer (Dan 9:20–24) and Habakkuk's prayer (Hab 2:3).

Third, God gives such *liberal* answers (Jas 1:5, 6; Eph 3:20). He doesn't stint in his supply or first make a minute interrogation of our motives and our worthiness.

Privileged for Accessible Grace

Fourth, God's gracious desire for answering prayer is referenced by his fame in doing *great things* in answer to prayer. Edwards cites many Old Testament exploits wrought as a direct consequence of prayer.

Fifth, as he did with Jacob at Peniel, God can come out as if he were against us only to apparently change in his attitude and graciously be for us. The view that prayer changes things by *overcoming God*, as it were, was not a theological problem for Edwards's unflinching convictions on divine sovereignty: he staunchly believed God knows and appoints all things.

It is noteworthy that many of the examples I presented earlier in this book, which I suggested were capable of being seen as examples of unanswered prayer, Edwards appeals to in the most positive light as examples that fortify the fact that God answers prayer. So much, then, does depend on the perspective we have. Do we set out with the perspective that God is harsh, unfair, eager to use his right as God to disappoint us, to go silent on us when we are most desperate? Or are we primarily disposed to knowing God as full of grace and love? For Edwards, there was no competition; the perspective had to be one of grace. Scripturally, that is where our perspective should lie as well.

Hard thoughts of God have always been the tendency of the fallen: a predisposition to question God's integrity. Adam and Eve first came to grief in Eden over this—an environment with potential for the greatest experience of happiness and communion with God, all blighted, ruined by a harsh perspective, fed by lies, of hard thoughts of God (Gen 3:1–13). The thoughts of the redeemed should be different—"whatever is true, whatever is honourable, whatever is just, whatever is pure, whatever is lovely, whatever is commendable, if there is any excellence, if there is anything worthy of praise, think about these things" (Phil 4:8). This should be our perspective, for this is where the scriptural testimony and that supplied overwhelmingly by countless Christians down through the ages lies in regard to God's character.

So, when we are about to complain of an unanswered prayer, should we not first compose ourselves and think, "Is it not a wonderful thing that I can even approach God at all? What a wonderful place the throne of grace is! This is the closest to paradise on earth, where I can come to actually meet with God! This sublime place, where God so encourages me to come; where he *wants* me to come more than ever I could want to come. Having encouraged me and invited me to come, is he likely to reverse his opinion when I do come—to spite me? Will such a God 'pull a fast one on me' and choose to ignore me, or worse, not show up at all? Surely, a thousand times 'no'! His grace never cheats on the people he loves!" As Jesus reminds us, it is unthinkable that if we ask for bread our heavenly father will cheat us with a stone (Matt 7:7–11).

As I was reviewing this chapter I happened to listen to a radio dramatization of Lucy Caldwell's stage play *Note to Future Self*. The play is about a thirteen-year-old girl, whose one-time hippy mother gives her the name Philosophy Rainbow—Sophie, for short—after she is diagnosed with a terminal illness. She is housed by her grandmother, Daphne, in Birmingham, along with the mother, Judy, and her sister, Calliope. At one very moving point in the play Calliope tells Daphne, a very religious woman, that she should not pray for Sophie anymore; in fact, she hates those prayers. Daphne is shocked and tries to remonstrate with Calliope until the girl spits out a prayer actually based on the words of Jesus in John 14:13, "Whatsoever you ask in my name, this I will do, that the Father may be glorified in the Son. If you ask me anything in my name, I will do it." So Calliope shouts and sobs out, to the God she no longer believes in, her request that God, whom she asks in Jesus' name, would heal her dear sister. One cannot but be deeply moved by this cry of desperation that was not granted in the end. What Lucy Caldwell captures so vividly is what many have anguished over in similar circumstances; but not all have taken so violent a perspective on what God is like as Calliope did, and they have coped differently than her. So much can depend on the relationship we have developed with God before the crisis, because if we wait for the crisis to come first the relationship may never cope.

A configured relationship may convince us that God is not obliged to us in any way outside what he has promised to be to us; but that he has promised to be so much to us in regard to prayer is surely our highest honor. In prayer the honor is all ours. God is not ennobled by our prayers, but we are, beyond doubt. It is not so much a problem that God doesn't answer some of our prayers; it is a wonder that he answers any. But, because of his grace, he answers *so* many.

Add to the ingredients of God's grace the fact that he is so ready to answer our prayers; that he will never ignore any plea made in Christ's name; that he delights to answer liberally; that he will do great things by our prayers; and that he will even seem to override himself to these ends, and we can see how wonderful and encouraging are the starting blocks for prayer. To choose any other starting place is to choose a hard place, so out of place with the grace we have had lavished upon us.

Just imagine being among those members of Jonathan Edwards's church as they waited, day by day, to see who that silent, virulent bug, progressing at epidemic speed through their neighborhoods, would strike next. You have no vaccine, no antibiotics—nothing to save you at all if it infects you. At the next muscle ache or sneeze or stomach cramp, your anxiety level rises. How do you think you would cope? I know how people feel under marginally less severe conditions; I have witnessed it with my own eyes and ears in Haiti, with the cholera that can kill within three hours, but that at least is curable if help is sought in time. Imagine no cure at all. Which is the best foothold to have in those circumstances? To be stuck in your hard thoughts of a God who you feel has let you down because he hasn't yet answered your prayer to your expectations? Just a few in Haiti did start there, alas, already disappointed and embittered by the loss of loved ones or of houses during the prior earthquake, but not many I listened to did. Is it preferable, then, to be trusting in a God who has revealed so much of his love and grace to you *in Christ*, and who has provided open access to himself, let alone whatever he can give you in addition? There is no such place as a throne of grace where God doesn't show up.

So, as we are tempted to complain of prayer unanswered, we should think, in Jonathan Edwards's words, "Hence we may know how we are *privileged*, in that we have the Most High revealed to us, who is a God that heareth prayer. The greater part of mankind are destitute of this privilege. Whatever their necessities are, whatever their calamities or sorrows, they have no prayer-hearing God to whom they may go."[2] People without the privilege of prayer can only hang on superstitious rituals; mutter faithless words in a panic into the ether to whoever or whatever may be there to hear; burst into tears in the hope that these faithless words may move the heart of a deity they do not know and have never been interested in until the crisis hit them; or sink into the depths of hopeless despair for want of anything they can do or say that will make any difference. Thank God, that is not how it ever is for a Christian! Whatever our emergency—maybe a crisis of health, some terrible diagnosis or disabling injury; maybe a heartbreaking disintegration of a relationship; maybe a failure to gain some necessary exam grades; maybe being trapped in some violent or empty relationship, or in a theatre of war—whatever it is, we have a resort we can immediately

2. Ibid., 116.

go to, to find grace to help in time of need—a place where we can pour out whatever is on our heart, and then trust in amazing grace!

Deep down in every human being's heart, I believe, there is a longing for such a resort, and a secret envy of the Christian who clearly has it and makes use of it. So blessed are we with the privilege!

However, in regard to the Christian's life of prayer there is even more to be encouraged by.

15

A Prayer that Cannot Go Unanswered!

THERE IS A PARTICULAR CATEGORY to the biblical doctrine of prayer that is often overlooked, especially when it comes to the problem of unanswered prayer. Yet, it is arguably the most encouraging to be found in Christian belief and practice, and another of the staggering outcomes of the seemingly unanswered prayer of Jesus in the Garden of Gethsemane and while on the cross! A theologian has described this work as one the apostles spoke of with "adoring awe," because "it seemed to have impressed them as one of the unimaginable wonders of redemption—something which in love went far beyond all that we could ask or think."[1]

When we become so preoccupied by the problem of unanswered prayer we can tend to the view that perhaps God doesn't answer prayer after all, and for that reason prayer can become redundant in the Christian's life. That is a disappointing outcome to unanswered prayer. As a counterpart to any notions of unanswered prayer, therefore, we need to be aware of a praying that goes on continually on our behalf, specific to our needs, which cannot go unanswered by God. I refer to the teaching in Scripture concerning the work of Christ as our high priest in heaven, who ever lives to make intercession for us, as disclosed in statements such as "since he always lives to make intercession for them" (Heb 7:25) and "who indeed is interceding for us" (Rom 8:34). In both these references the context adds encouragement to the underlying truth.

---

1. Mackintosh, *Doctrine of the Person of Jesus Christ*, 376.

Hello? Is Anyone There?

The writer to the Hebrews was presenting Jesus Christ as coming in the order of, yet as much superior to, the Old Testament priestly figure of Melchizedek. Christ is superior by virtue of his indestructible life, his being the guarantor of a better covenant, and because of the fact that, unlike the Old Testament priests, who needed replacing when they died, he "always lives to make intercession for [us]." Under the Old Testament covenant arrangements, if one's prayer was not answered, one could use the sheer mortality of the high priest, through whom one prayed, as a possible reason for that prayer going unanswered. But, now, under the New Testament covenant arrangement, any such reasoning is invalid, since the risen and ascended Christ never ceases to make intercession for us. So, while we Christians are complaining to God of his not answering our prayers, the Son of God is interceding for us in prayer in a ministry that never ceases! This ministry is such that, to quote John Calvin, "we may confidently come to [God], and with such an intercessor, trusting nothing we ask in his name will be denied us, as nothing can be denied to him by the Father."[2]

Now, in the Romans context the Apostle Paul was addressing believers who were enduring great suffering and, therefore, circumstances almost guaranteed to create doubt as to God's power for, or knowledge of, his people and their very salvation. So, to confirm the impossibility of there being any condemnation for the Christian, the apostle draws upon the assurance from Christ's death, his resurrection, his ascension, and his intercession; he hammers four nails, as it were, into the coffin of a Christian's doubts regarding her salvation! Consequently, while we Christians worry whether God's silences are indicative of our being regarded as outside of salvation or of God's being unmindful of our life-and-death struggles, all the while the Son of God is praying for us with these very things in mind!

There is no doubt that the issue of unanswered prayer can expose the dysfunctional way we run prayer at times. For example, it may be that we hit a particular crisis point in our lives—it may be a health issue, since these issues do affect us very deeply. Let us pretend that we become aware of a health issue. So, we pray for God to intervene, which usually means we desire to be healed. But nothing happens; our health remains just as poor, or we get worse. So, we pray more often, and with more passion. But, again, nothing happens to heal us. After a while, perhaps after a time of soul-searching to ensure there is nothing we can find that would be an obvious

2. Calvin, *Institutes of the Christian Religion*, 874.

A Prayer that Cannot Go Unanswered!

reason for God not to answer our prayer, we become panicky, and then resentful that God will not hear us.

Perhaps such scenarios reveal more about us than about God. They reveal a dysfunctional approach to prayer and to God—a rather "device-like" approach. Our confidence in him as someone worthy of knowing and trusting is measured by the speed with which he responds to our felt needs and emergencies—that is, to heal us. If we are younger rather than older, of if we have young children or grandchildren, we assume our right to live a long life, to see our children or grandchildren grow up. Anything that infringes upon such an assumption cannot be right. So, any failure of God to put health issues right cannot be right! But, from what Bible can we draw such assumptions?

So, where does the fact of Christ's constant intercession for the Christian come into this perspective? Is God more likely to be persuaded by our panic (unbelief) than by the profound prayers of his Son, who loves us more than we can ever imagine? Surely not. The Pray-er whose prayers cannot go unanswered should be the all-time panic-stopper for desperate Christians.

Without Christ ascended and glorified in heaven as our great high priest there would be no answered prayer whatsoever. As it is, all our prayers go through the filter of Christ as our mediator, our prayer partner, and the appropriate prayers are presented to the Father in a manner that cannot be refused.

We do not have any right whatsoever to assume we are so important, or so qualified, to demand or deserve the hearing and answering of God. The exhortation for Christians to approach the throne of grace with confidence (Heb 4:16) does not provide for that kind of assumption. The disposition of God as one who hears prayer (Ps 65:2) is a disposition of sheer grace, not of our desert. We must never forget this. Sometimes the impression can be given by some that because we are mere creatures, small and lacking in awareness and knowledge in comparison with God, then just that huge disjunction between God and us humans should present us with an intuitive assumption that we have a right to be heard by God. That is a false assumption, from a biblical and theological perspective. Such an assumption was forfeited at the fall, when the first humans refused to listen and obey when God spoke to them, and they were excluded from Eden. From then on the only route to the ear of God must be through Christ, the Mediator (1 Tim 2:5). That we now have the status we do have in Christ is nothing short of breathtaking in terms of grace and privilege. All the promises of

God regarding prayer are *promises* because they take their bearings from the intercession of Christ as our mediator and high priest.

Surely then, from this great work of Christ we can conclude that whenever God seems to be silent, neglectful, or dismissive of the most urgent pleas of our prayers, there is a need to exert an active faith in the truth that the Son of God is always interceding for us? Every desire we make known, every word we utter, every tear that falls, is noticed and taken on board by this great intercessor and mediator, to whom our interests and cares are uppermost. In the practice of lament we can go to Jesus in prayer, reminding him that he too has known this kind of struggle that we are having—calling on God out of our broken hearts and God now seeming not to hear! He too has suffered the same, even though in the case of his prayers it is unthinkable he could not be heard.

In addition to this, we can also conclude, even when we give up praying, Christ carries on for us!

Sometimes Christians can become desperate when it comes to praying—desperately worried that maybe they are not praying enough. For instance, they may fear that because their poor health or physical degeneration makes it very difficult for them to sustain praying for long, perhaps their weakness is a handicap to effectual praying. And if their prayers seem to go unanswered, then maybe this is why—they just aren't praying enough, or in the right way or attitude. Some folk have almost been driven crazy by such thoughts. The fact is that God understands our weakness, and when illness or injury or shock so debilitate us so that we just cannot summon the energy for prayer, Christ, our intercessor, carries on praying for us with cries that cannot be denied.

Of course, it is always good for individual Christians to have other Christians supporting them in prayer, especially when they feel weakened. Sometimes it seems that it is the sheer number of people praying, and the combined force of their pleas, that moves the heart of God to respond. In reality, however, it is the raising of our needs by Christ as intercessor with God that is the reason for any and every prayer being heard and answered.

But, finally, how should we understand this business of Christ always interceding for us? How ought we to conceive of this?

We should not think of him having to beg, plead, or wrestle, as we might. Christ does not have to continue to, as it were, sweat great drops of blood (Luke 22:44). Nor will the Son have any caution about whether or not he will be heard, whether or not his request is valid, timely, or in keeping with the will of God; rather, the mere presentation of himself, as the God-Man, with his perfect righteousness and his shed blood, and the sharing of his heart in that perfect union with the Father, is enough for the Father to ensure he will hear him. As Mackintosh expresses it, "Theirs is a unity that needs no language."[3] Even so, this still includes the idea of Christ actually formulating petitions to the Father.

Surely the intercessory work of Christ is not meant to reduce our own desire for prayer, but it is a most potent fact that can minimize our anxiety during times of unanswered prayer. The Greek verb used in Rom 8:26–27, εντυγχανει, carries the sense of asking, petitioning. So it is more than simply Christ being present; he does represent our needs verbally, as well as visually (in the form of the sacrificial Lamb of God).

So, this ongoing role of Christ our saviour has to be a significant facet within our theology and practice of prayer, albeit one that is so often overlooked when we are in the mood to complain. It is integral also to the promise of Christ that here on earth, immersed in our sufferings and inner and outer conflicts, we are not left alone, as orphans (John 14:18). The Holy Spirit is with us, and he too prays for us during these awful times: "Likewise the Spirit helps us in our weakness. For we do not know what to pray for as we ought, but the Spirit himself intercedes for us with groanings too deep for words. And he who searches the heart knows what is the mind of the Spirit, because the Spirit intercedes for the saints according to the will of God" (Rom 8:26–27).

The risen and ascended Christ, the indwelling Holy Spirit—these are the respondents to the hard thoughts of God not answering our prayers! Christ and the Spirit have never ceased to pray for us in our troubles, and these petitions can never be denied, for these all fit the essential criterion, namely, according to the will of God.

---

3. Mackintosh, *Doctrine of the Person of Jesus Christ*, 377.

16

The Final Answer—"Trust Me!"

THIS BOOK HAS ATTEMPTED TO provide a practical theology for addressing the problem of unanswered prayer. In so doing we started by outlining some kinds of prayer that God has explicitly stated he cannot answer, and it needs to be our discipline not to engage in such prayers. Next, we have sought to clarify what we mean by unanswered prayer, and we have worked with a definition that has, by and large, been constructed very much from our own perspective, rather than a scriptural perspective. The reason for this has been, very simply, because that is the way we often see and feel the problem, which is the point where I wished to begin my focus in this book, so I could attempt to scratch where it itches, so to speak. A further development was to reflect on certain Old and New Testament passages that touch on the matter of unanswered prayer, thus gauging the extent to which the Bible recognizes unanswered prayer as a problem and how it affects those characters involved. From this we have drawn observations from these reflections that proffer practical help directly to the problem. Then, finally, we have ensured we reflect on the overall beauty and privilege of prayer and the need to focus upon this above the problematic aspects. The most encouraging stimuli to engaging in such a positive exercise must be the wonder of our free access to the throne of grace and the corresponding demand for trusting God, and also the fact of Christ and the Holy Spirit never ceasing to pray effectively for us.

It remains, therefore, for me to press home a conclusion as being the single one that is incumbent upon us for addressing the problem of

The Final Answer—"Trust Me!"

unanswered prayer—trusting the Answerer, who sometimes doesn't seem to answer.

An incident involving Jesus and his disciples offers some real help to us. You can read it in Mark 4:36–41: Jesus' so-called stilling of the storm.

Jesus had proposed that, together, he and his disciples should take a boat trip across the Sea of Galilee, all the way to the other side. Incidentally, that part of the drama must not be overlooked: "Let us go across *to the other side*" (Mark 4:35, emphasis mine). That was the Master's plan.

As they were sailing a strong storm arose, which began filling the boat with water to such an extent that these seasoned seafarers and fishermen were afraid they would drown. The way Mark narrates things, very likely from the disciple Peter's recall of the incident, leaves the reader actually feeling the fear and blind panic that was aboard that boat at the time! In their crisis the disciples went to call on Jesus for help and discovered he was fast asleep in the back of the boat! At the moment they needed him most urgently, he was asleep. They eventually managed to wake him up, however, and he stilled the storm before challenging them with the words, "Why are you so afraid? Have you still no faith?" (Mark 4:40).

Now, in this incident we do not have an unanswered prayer as such, not even a prayer in the sense we usually understand it. However, we do have a critical incident and a conversation between some disciples and Jesus as Son of God. In that sense it is a realistic enactment of what goes on in much petitionary prayer—people in crisis pleading with God—and I appeal to it for that reason as we reflect upon the significance of faith in regard to addressing the problem of unanswered prayer. I don't believe it is stretching a point to do so.

This was not a random journey, something cooked up by Jesus at the end of a busy day. It had an explicitly stated purpose—to go across to the other side of the lake. It was rich with an implicit purpose as well—namely, helping those disciples, and all Christians subsequently, understand certain things about life as a disciple of Jesus Christ for when Jesus in the flesh would be no longer literally at hand. That is why I believe it offers some help in both understanding what may be happening in some instances of unanswered prayer and in how to cope with such.

First of all, in regard to life, this narrative implants on our hearts the view that *our life is far from stable, and we are far from indomitable*. Every one of us loves stability in life, the relaxing thought that we can plan a day and actually have some feel-good confidence that we will live to see those plans fulfilled. They may be plans for travel to work, to do the work we have planned, or to have a lie-in. They may be plans to visit family or relatives. They may be plans for a glorious holiday. They may be plans for entering retirement. We have so many plans, don't we? Yet, the reality is that a day can start out as the happiest day of your life and then, suddenly, turn into the worst day of your life, the direst nightmare. It can happen to anyone, at any time, and no one can afford to think, "It won't be for me!" Life is so much bigger, more out of our control, more ferocious at times, than we are able to handle at our most strong and wise. The trouble is that our sophistication and advanced capacity for organizing and fixing things in life can delude us into assuming we are safer than we actually are.

This is why we should never go a day without walking with God and trusting in his providence. The very thought, "I don't have any need of actively inviting God into my plans and routine today" should be unthinkable to us. When the Apostle James was warning people against praying selfishly for God to fulfill their personal greed, he also took them to task for leaving God out of their plans (Jas 4:13–17). Imagine: praying for God to help you fulfill a particular desire for a plan, but having no desire for God to intervene in any other way! Of course, no one would verbalize it quite like this: "God, get me out of this hole, then you can go back to bed!" But that is what the attitude amounts to. That was what those people in James' day were, in effect, wanting. They had their personal business plans, which they rehearsed from day to day: "Today or tomorrow we will go into such and such a town and spend a year there and trade and make a profit" (Jas 4:13). That statement betrays how confident these businesspeople were.

But how absurd an outlook if life in general, in every place, is actually more like it was on Lake Galilee—if, in an instant, some crisis might blow up and threaten everything. How right James was to remind us, "Yet you do not know what tomorrow will bring. What is your life? For you are a mist that appears for a little time and then vanishes" (Jas 4:14). Yes, that is, from one perspective, *all* we are—at our fittest, wisest, most skilled and astute—a mist! And we are still as much today, with the passing of two thousand years since James wrote those words, despite all the inventions, discoveries, and technological and healthcare advances we have made that seem to make life safer. This is why it is right we ought to say, "If the Lord wills, we will live and do this or that." And to function each day with this perspective we need to live in a prayerful mode. That is why we are exhorted to "be constant in prayer" (Rom 12:12), to "not be anxious about anything, but in

The Final Answer—"Trust Me!"

everything by prayer and thanksgiving let [our] requests be made known unto God" (Phil 4:6), and to "continue steadfastly in prayer" (Col 4:2). Throughout each day it is possible, and necessary, to live on two integrated levels. One is the level of our day-to-day life: our family, our work, our personal life; in other words, the level of this world amid all its demands and crises. The other is the level of accessible grace at the throne of grace. In this sense it is very possible to live with a foot in both camps. In fact, it is exactly how a Christian should live! The life of grace, giving open access to God, is designed for the way life in this world really is. In this sense, the fallen, unstable world and divine grace are totally compatible for the full functioning of grace. No one can say that the grace of a life of prayer just cannot function in this unstable, real world, or, to put it another way, that prayer cannot cope with the realities of life today.

However, the Galilee incident also reminds us that when crises arise, and we are in the mode of prayer, *it can seem that God is asleep.* Just when the disciples wanted and needed him most, Jesus was "asleep on the cushion" (Mark 4:38). That is how it is sometimes in our own experience, isn't it? When the deepest crisis we have ever had to face blows up in our faces, we may well pray as we have never prayed before—with such strength, with such urgency, even with such blind fear. But God seems to be asleep!

So, what ought we to do? How ought we to carry ourselves, as it were, when in a crisis and when God seems to be fast asleep? I am asking myself this as I reread the details of this incident in Mark 4. Jesus asks the disciples, "Why are you so afraid?" On the one hand, I must admit that sounds a bit of a daft question to ask when you are in a little boat in the middle of a storm with the boat sinking! On the other hand, it is *the* question to ask yourself as a Christian: "*Why* am I afraid?"

Fear, or anxiety, is very often a key feature in the problem of unanswered prayer. Without an answer we become increasingly anxious and fearful. One way to address this is to ask the question Jesus did: "Why?" Not "Why is God doing this to me?" or "Why has this happened?" but, "Why am I afraid?"

In my work with trauma survivors, high levels of anxiety and fear figure very often in the people I see. Sometimes I do a very practical exercise with them. I call it "peeling the onion of fear." We do it on a piece of paper, in fact. I get them to write down in a single short sentence at the top of the page what their anxiety or fear is. So, for example, we can imagine one of the disciples in the boat writing, "I got seriously fearful when the storm overwhelmed us." I then ask the question, "Why?" and get them to write down a reason. This disciple may write, "Because Jesus was asleep!" So I follow this with another question: "Why did that fact make you afraid?" To which he might reply, "Because there was a terrible storm." So I continue to ask, "And why did that make you afraid?" He might reply, "Because I feared the boat would sink." So then I might ask a question like this, "And if the boat did sink, why would that worry you?" He might write next (after looking at me as if I were stupid!), "Because I could not swim very far in that kind of storm!" So I continue: "And why would that make you so scared!" And the reply could come back, "I am afraid I would drown!" And so I would go on, asking "Why?" after each answer, until we had gotten to the very core of this fear, to the most basic reason, which might well be "Because I don't want to die" or "Because I love my family and am not ready to die." The thing is, whatever the basic reason may be, I guarantee the answer to it will lie totally outside of our control, except through hoping or trusting in something. From a Christian perspective, the only way of resolving that basic fear will be to trust God as your friend, trust that he is in good control. As the Apostle John put it, "There is no fear in love, but perfect love casts out fear" (1 John 4:18). This is why Jesus asked his disciples, "Have you still no faith?"

In our pleading with God for an answer to our prayers for help, in our anxiety and fear over obtaining a clear answer, the time comes to stop that frenzy of pleading, that panic, and just trust—just realize that we have placed the matter in God's hands, believing he is who he is—God—and we are who we are—his children. We have to leave it there; we have to just get on with our living. There is no more we can do. Beating ourselves up over perhaps not praying enough or rightly, not using the right posture or place or words, is futile to obtaining peace and conquering anxiety. We have to trust God. Now doing that in the peak of a storm at sea cannot be easy, I grant you; but it is what Jesus was advocating no less. After all, what was the alternative except just increasing panic? Trust and hope in God is far better! This is what the Apostle Paul meant when he taught, "The Lord is at hand; do not be anxious about anything, but in everything by prayer and supplication with thanksgiving let your requests be made known to God. And the peace of God, which surpasses all understanding, will guard your hearts and your minds in Christ Jesus" (Phil 4:5–7).

Being born and brought up in Cornwall, by the sea, and by a father who loved both boats and being on the sea, I was introduced to boats and the sea very early on in my life. Until my early thirties, however, I could not swim! I never had the courage to learn. I had a fear of holding my head underwater for some reason. It was during that "I can't swim" phase that I read some of the journals of the Methodist leader and evangelist John Wesley. I read of an occasion when, prior to his conversion, Wesley was on a sailing ship crossing the Atlantic Ocean. An almighty storm blew up (as often happened) and threatened the survival of the boat, her crew, and the passengers. The sea at one point came over the ship, split the mainsail in pieces, and poured all over and into the ship between the decks. This was accompanied by great screams from among the English passengers, and Wesley himself admitted he was utterly terrified. However, as all this was going on, Wesley noticed some German passengers, who were Moravian Christian missionaries, remaining at peace and carrying on singing hymns! After the storm had subsided, Wesley spoke to the Moravians' leader. "Were you not afraid?" he asked. The man replied, "I thank God, no." So Wesley asked, "Were not your women and children afraid?" and the man replied again, "No, our women and children are not afraid to die."

At the root of so many fears and so much anxiety lies the basic fear of dying, and the prayers we make want God to prevent our dying. That is not how it seems at first; we have other reasons, to be sure. But when fear is peeled back to the core, the fear of death is almost always there. That was just how it was for the disciples.

Yet the prayer never to die is the one prayer we can guarantee God will more than likely not answer! As far as we know, only two human beings have not had to go through the process of dying, Enoch and Elijah, and only those who are alive when Christ returns will never die in the future. Everyone else, no matter how healthy, holy, or evil, has had to die or will have to die. With all due respect to the teaching of Scripture that Christians need to have hope in Christ's return, it was never intended as a substitute for coming to terms with death. So, the assumption remains, we all have to face dying, and we have little control over the circumstances in which our dying may take place. It may be while surrounded by our family, in the hospital or in the comfort of our home, with the best palliative care there is on hand to ensure pain and suffering are kept at bay; or it may be at sea in a storm or during a grounding, and a capsize and sinking amid suffering and fear. But whatever the circumstances, until this basic fear is resolved before God we will never have real peace, and we will be forever at risk from unresolved unanswered prayer and the anxiety it stokes in times of crisis.

Resolving the fear of death or dying can only be done through faith in Jesus Christ and trusting God. That kind of trust that comes from knowing God and loving God because, remember, "Perfect loves casts out fear" (1 John 4:18).

In Scripture death is described as "the last enemy" (1 Cor 15:26), and it is the risen and ascended Christ who shall bring about the final defeat (Rev 20:14). It is, therefore, our trusting in Jesus Christ as Savior and Lord that guarantees defeat of, and deliverance from, this last enemy: "Since therefore the children share in flesh and blood, he himself likewise partook of the same things, that through death he might destroy the one who has the power of death, that is, the devil, and deliver all those who through fear of death were subject to lifelong slavery" (Heb 2:14–15).

So, coming back to the question, what should these disciples have done? They ought to have realized that the safest place they could have been that day was right where they were—in that storm, on that sinking boat, along with even a *sleeping* Jesus! They were safer there than all those people who were ashore, without Jesus.

Sometimes, when we have prayed our eyes dry and wrung our hearts out and God still seems to remain asleep, we have to just stop panicking and trust, because we are in the safest place right where we are—where, if he deems it for the best, the storms are at their worst. And then to remember that even the wind and the sea obey him, so whatever happens, he will not lose control of our good. The final answer from the Answerer of unanswered prayer is "Trust Me!" If for the moment we get no other response from God, we have this one at least. There is *never* total silence.

Bibliography

Beck, Peter. *The Voice of Faith: Jonathan Edwards's Theology of Prayer*. Guelph, ON: Joshua Press, 2010.
Benson, Herbert. *Timeless Healing: The Power and Biology of Belief*. New York: Scribner, 1996.
Calvin, John. *Commentary on the Book of Psalms*. Translated by James Anderson. Vol. 2. Grand Rapids: Baker, 1979.
———. *Institutes of the Christian Religion*. Edited by John T. McNeill. Translated by Ford Lewis Battles. Vol. 2. Philadelphia: Westminster, 1960.
Candlish, Robert S. *Studies in Genesis*. Grand Rapids: Kregel, 1979.
Carson, D. A. *A Call to Spiritual Reformation: Priorities from Paul and His Prayers*. Grand Rapids: Baker, 1992.
Dunn, Ronald. *Don't Just Stand There . . . Pray Something! Discover the Incredible Power of Intercessory Prayer*. Amersham, UK: Alpha, 1995.
Edwards, Jonathan. "The Most High a Prayer-Hearing God." Sermon 4 in *The Works of Jonathan Edwards*, revised and corrected by Edward Hickman, 2:113–18. Edinburgh: Banner of Truth Trust, 1974.
Forsyth, Peter Taylor. *The Justification of God*. Studies in Theology. London: Duckworth, 1916.
Fretheim, Terence E. *Creation Untamed: The Bible, God, and Natural Disasters*. Grand Rapids: Baker Academic, 2010.
Fyall, Robert S. *Now My Eyes Have Seen You: Images of Creation and Evil in the Book of Job*. Downers Grove, IL: Apollos, 2002.
Goodwin, Thomas. *The Return of Prayers*. London: printed by R. H. for R. Dawlman, 1659. Kindle edition.
Greig, Peter. *God on Mute: Engaging the Problem of Unanswered Prayer*. Ventura, CA: Regal, 2007.
Grudem, Wayne. *Systematic Theology: An Introduction to Biblical Doctrine*. Leicester: InterVarsity, 1994.
Hart, David Bentley. *The Doors of the Sea: Where Was God in the Tsunami?* Grand Rapids: Eerdmans, 2005.
Helm, Paul. *The Providence of God*. Contours of Christian Theology. Downers Grove, IL: InterVarsity, 1993.
Koenig, Harold G., et al. *Handbook of Religion and Health*. New York: Oxford University Press, 2001.
Kuyper, Abraham. *To Be Near unto God*. Translated by John Hendrik de Vries. Grand Rapids: Baker, 1925.
Lewis, C. S. *A Grief Observed*. London: Faber & Faber, 1961.

Bibliography

Lloyd-Jones, D. Martyn. *From Fear to Faith: Studies in the Book of Habakkuk*. Leicester: InterVarsity, 1951.
Mackintosh, H. R. *The Doctrine of the Person of Jesus Christ*. Edinburgh: T. & T. Clark, 1913.
McGrath, Alister, ed. *The Blackwell Encyclopedia of Modern Christian Thought*. Malden, MA: Blackwell, 1993.
Peretti, Frank E. *This Present Darkness*. Wheaton, IL: Crossway, 2003.
Pert, Candace B. *Molecules of Emotion: Why You Feel the Way You Feel*. London: Schribner, 1998.
Pinnock, Clark H., ed. *The Grace of God, the Will of Man: The Case for Arminianism*. Grand Rapids: Zondervan 1990.
Piper, John. "Are There Two Wills in God?" In *Still Sovereign*, edited by Thomas R. Schreiner and Bruce A. Ware, 107–31. Grand Rapids: Baker, 2000.
Reinders, Hans. "Providence and Ethics." A conference paper presented for "*Deus Habet Consilium*: The Career and Prospects of Providence in Modern Theology," School of Divinity, History, and Philosophy, University of Aberdeen, January 2008.
Schreiner, Thomas R., and Bruce A. Ware, eds. *Still Sovereign: Contemporary Perspectives on Election, Foreknowledge, and Grace*. Grand Rapids: Baker, 2000.
Servan-Schreiber, David. *The Instinct to Heal: Curing Stress, Anxiety and Depression without Drugs and without Talk Therapy*. Emmaus, PA: Rodale, 2004.
Shuman, Joel James, and Keith G. Meador. *Heal Thyself: Spirituality, Medicine, and the Distortion of Christianity*. Oxford: Oxford University Press, 2003.
Sloane, Richard. *Blind Faith: The Unholy Alliance of Religion and Medicine*. New York: St. Martin's Griffin, 2006.
Stott, John. *The Cross of Christ*. 2nd ed. Leicester: InterVarsity, 1989.
Surin, Kenneth. "The Problem of Evil." In *The Blackwell Encyclopedia of Modern Christian Thought*, edited by Alister McGrath, 192–99. Oxford: Blackwell, 1993.
Tutu, Desmond. *No Future Without Forgiveness*. London: Rider, 1999.
Vanhoozer, Kevin J. *The Drama of Doctrine: A Canonical Linguistic Approach to Christian Theology*. Louisville: Westminster John Knox, 2005.
Volf, Miroslav. *Exclusion and Embrace: A Theological Exploration of Identity, Otherness, and Reconciliation*. Nashville: Abingdon, 1996.
Webster, John. "On the Theology of Providence." A conference paper presented for "*Deus Habet Consilium*: The Career and Prospects of Providence in Modern Theology," School of Divinity, History, and Philosophy, University of Aberdeen, January 2008.
Yancey, Philip. *Prayer: Does It Make a Difference?* London: Hodder & Stoughton, 2006.

Scripture Reference Index

Genesis

3:1–13	97
3:5–6	73–74
3:10	86
11:30	91
12:1–3	91
15:1–3, 5	91
16:1–6	92
17:1–2	92
18:12–14	92
18:25	83
21:1	92
22:2	93
25:22–26, 29–34	26
27:1–40	26
32:7–18, 22–26	26–27
32:22–32	25
32:30	27
37–41	55–56
45:5, 8	56
50:20	56

Exodus

2:23–24	10
14:10–12, 15	14

Deuteronomy

1:37	22
29	66
29:18–19, 20–28	66
29:29	2, 71

1 Samuel

8:1–18	10

2 Samuel

7:1–17	30
12:16–23	22

1 Kings

18:26–29	xiv
19:11–12	77

1 Chronicles

17:1–17	30–33
17:23–27	33

Nehemiah

2:4	28

Job

2:9	28
7:12–21	52
13:15	87
16:11–14	52
10:6–20	28
38–41	76
40–41	34
40:4	65
42:2	87
42:7	52

Scripture Reference Index

Psalms

10	46
13	46
13:1–2	56
22	46
25:1–3, 21	55
27	55
35	46
40:2	11
42:5	76
44	46
65:2	4, 96, 103
66	9
66:19	11
69	46
88	46
116:1–2	xvi
130	55–56
139	75, 77

Isaiah

1:10–17	12
1:15	8, 50
38:12–14	28
40:27–31	54–55
51:9	53
55:8–9	45, 94
58	12
62:6–7	52–53

Jeremiah

32	78–79

Lamentations

3:3–10	28
3:39–45	11
3:44	50

Daniel

9–10	35
9:20–24	96

Hosea

12:3–4	26–27

Habakkuk

1–3	57–58
1:12–17	82
1:13	82
2:1	40
2:3	96
2:4	41, 67

Matthew

1:6	29
5–7	14–16
5:45	22
6	65
6:5–7	14
6:6	51
6:7–8	77
6:9	31
6:14–15	16
6:33	32
7:7–11	5, 98
13:13	1
17:20	17
18:21–35	16
20:21–23	22
26:39–42	59
27:42–46	46

Mark

4:36–41	107
4:35	107
4:38	109
9:5	32
9:7	86
11:24	5
12:1–11	86
13:32	65
14:36	87

116

Scripture Reference Index

LUKE

1:28–38	
2:4	29
2:22–38	92
11:1–13	4, 27
11:5–13	51
11:9–13	2
18:1–8	6
18:1–5	51
18:13	xiv
22:41–44	83
22:44	104

JOHN

2:19	33
3:16	22
4:24	34
14:13	5, 98
14:18	105
16:23–24	5

ACTS

16:6–7	32

ROMANS

1:17	67
3:26	85
5:5	74
5:8, 10	22
8:15–16	74
8:19	7
8:26, 28	60
8:26–27	105
8:28–30	61–62
8:34	101–2
11	74
11:33	74
12:12	6, 108

1 CORINTHIANS

1:2,3	96
1:18–31	67
1:20–31	83
3:16	33
10:11	38
15:26	112

2 CORINTHIANS

9:18	22
11:30	37
12:1–10	36–38
12:11	39

GALATIANS

4:4	92
5:17	9–10

EPHESIANS

3	63
3:14–21	29
3:20–21	74
3:20	92, 96
5:17	73
6:18	6, 34

PHILIPPIANS

1:6	10
4:5–7	110
4:6	23, 109
4:8	97

COLOSSIANS

4:2	109

1 THESSALONIANS

5:7	6

1 TIMOTHY

2:5	103

2 TIMOTHY

3:16–17	72

Scripture Reference Index

Hebrews

2:14–15	112
4:14, 16	96
4:15	81
4:16	103
7:25	101–2
11:11–12	92
11:18–19	94

James

1:1–17	18–19
1:5	5
1:5–6	96
1:17	22
4:3	27
4:3, 16	19
4:13–17	108
5:10	79
5:15	5
5:16–18	67

1 Peter

2:5	33
3:7	17

1 John

1:3	74
1:5	74, 82
1:6–10	9–10
1:7	74
1:8, 10	9
2:1	29
4:10	44
4:18	110, 112
5:14	73

Revelation

6:10	2
12	35
20:14	112

Subject and Author Index

Abraham and Sarah, 83, 91
  promise of son, 91–93
  sacrifice of son, 93–94
Adam and Eve, 73–74, 97
Annunciation, the, 80
apartheid, 17

Babylonian
  conquest, 57
  exile, 10–11
  siege of Jerusalem, 78
Baruch, 78
Beck, Peter, 80, 87
Behemoth, 34
Benson, Herbert, xiii
bereavement, xv
Bible study, 34

Caldwell, Lucy
  Note to Future Self, 98
Calvin, John, 10, 102
Candlish, Robert, 28
Carson, Donald A., 29
Christian marriage, 17–18
Christie, Agatha, 65
church
  birth of, 33
  in Corinth, 37
Cleese, John, 48

Daniel, 34–36
David, 22, 61
  desire to build temple, 29–33
  House of, 33
demonic spirits, 34–36
divine
  secrets, 71–74
  silence, 23–24

Dunn, Ronald, 53

earthquake, 2004 Indian Ocean, 83
Edwards, Jonathan, 77, 80, 82, 95–100
election, doctrine of, 74
Elijah, 6, 67, 77, 111
Enoch, 111
epidemic
  Boston MA 1735–36, 95–100
  Haiti 2010–11, 69–70, 76, 95–100
Esau, 25–27
evil, the problem of, 82–84
exile, the, 33, 35
Exodus, the, 14

Fall, the, 103
fasting, 34
Father Christmas, 21–22
fear of death, 110–12
forgiveness, 16
Forsyth, Peter T., 85
Fox, Matthew, 86
free will, 81
Fretheim, Terence, 88
friendship with God, 4
Fyall, Robert, 35

Gabriel, archangel, 80
genocide, 17
Gnosticism, 72
God
  as adversary, 26–29, 51–53
  the Answerer, 65, 82–89, 112
  appearing asleep, 46, 53
  cares, 76
  covenant, 66, 72
  Creator, 54
  engaging with, 50

Subject and Author Index

everlasting, 54
faithful, 43–44, 97–98
giver, the, 22
generosity, 96
grace, 93–96
hears/answers prayer, 4–5, 65, 81, 84, 88–89, 90–96, 107, 112
Holy Spirit, 34, 105
invitation, 97
judgment, 58
light, 74
mysteriousness, 71–72, 94
omnipotence, 75–81, 82, 87
omniscience, 75–81, 87, 94
providential will, 59–62, 62–70
sovereignty, 81
tirelessness, 54
unfailing love, 44
wisdom, 73–74, 83
Goodwin, Thomas, 42
gospel, the, 86
grace
   God's priority of, 95
   privilege of, 90–99
   sufficiency of, 37–38, 93–99
Greig, Peter, 6, 80, 87
Grudem, Wayne, 2

Habakkuk, 40, 57, 62, 82
Hagar, 92
Haiti earthquake, 2010, 4, 69–70, 76, 95
Hart, David Bentley, 34, 83–84
healers, 85
Helm, Paul, 62
Hezekiah, 28
hope in God, 55
human rights, 71

Isaac, 91–93
Jabbok, river, 27
   Jacob 25–28, 50
   at Peniel, 25–28, 50, 51, 97
   serves Laban, 26
   steals birthright, 26
James, apostle, 32, 79, 108
Jeremiah, 28, 35, 78
Jerusalem besieged, 78
Jesus
   on the cross, 46
   friend, 87–88
   in Gethsemane, xiv, 59, 82–83, 101
   intercedes for us, 101–5
   our mediator, 101–4
   Messiah, the, 92
   pre-incarnate appearance, 27, 35
   Savior, 86, 102, 105, 112
   Son of Man, 35
   stilling the storm, 107–10
   superior to Melchizedek, 102
   teaching on prayer, 2, 4, 5, 14, 65, 77
Job xiv, 28, 34–35, 52, 61, 62, 65, 76, 87
   friends, 57
   'patience', 53
John, apostle, 32
Joseph, 55, 59, 61

Koenig, Harold, xiv
Kuyper, Abraham, 50

lament, 45–49
Leviathan, 34
Lewis, Clive Staples xv, 60
Lloyd-Jones, D. Martyn, 40
Lot, 83

Mackintosh, H. R., 101, 105
Mary, 80
Meador, Keith G. xiv
meditation, 34
Melchizedek, 102
Michael, archangel, 35
Moses, 22, 93
mystery
   of the gospel, 63
   of providence, 63
mystery religions, 72
natural disasters, 88

Nathan, 30–33
Nehemiah, 28
Northern Ireland troubles, 17

Obsessive Compulsive Disorder (OCD), 43

Paul, apostle, 30, 61, 85, 102

Subject and Author Index

'thorn in the flesh', 36–39
Peretti, Frank, 35
Pert, Candace B., xiii
Peter, apostle, 32
Philippine flood 2011, 3–4
Pinnock, Clark H., 81
Piper, John, 73, 81
post-Enlightenment pride, 67, 84
postmodernism, 83
prayer
  according to God's will, 73
  answers to, 1, 42, 90
  being constant in, 108
  communion with God, 34
  delay in answer, 57–59
  ennobles us, 98
  expressing despair, 47
  free access to God, 96
  grace, invitation of, 94–100, 109
  as healthcare, xiii–xv, 43
  heartbreak in, 41–44
  impatience in, 45–47
  language of, 15, 45–49
  lessons of, 63
  liturgy, 43
  mystery of, 64
  perseverance in, 45, 51–53
  privilege of, 90–100
  as psychological comfort, 43
  relational, 4–5, 43, 64
  set prayers, 43
  for sick/suffering, 5–6
  spiritual warfare, 34–36
  storing up treasure, 65
  a struggle, 24–39
  unanswered, xv–xvii, 1–7, 40–44, 47–48, 51–52, 54–56, 57–62, 64–67, 69–70, 72–74, 77–79, 86–88, 90–95, 97–100, 101–5, 106–12
  as unfolding drama, 64
  waiting on God, 40–42, 54–60
  with eager longing, 7
prayer meetings, 15
prayers that God will not answer, 8–20
  goal to impress, 14–15
  mind divided, 18–19
  not properly asked, 19
  an unforgiving attitude, 16

  disobedience, 14
  sin cherished, 9–12
  social justice ignored, 12–14
prince of Persia, 35-6
psalmists, xiv

Rachel, 26
Rebekah, 26
Reinders, Hans, 73

sanctifying grace, 9
Scripture, canon of, 38
Scriven, Joseph, 88
St. Nicholas, 22
secrecy, 71
Sermon on the Mount, 14
Servan-Schreiber, David, xiii
Shuman, Joel James, xiv
Simeon and Anna, 92
Sloan, Richard, xiv
social justice, 12–14
Solomon, 33
Song of Songs, 44
songs of lament, 45–49
Spielberg, Steven, 65
Star Wars, 73
Stott, John R. W., 84
Surin, Kenneth, 84

Taiwan, visit to, 68–70
televangelists, 85
theodicy, 83
  philosophical, 83–85
  practical, 85–89
Timothy, 32
tough faith, 60–61
Transfiguration, Mount of, 32
trauma care, 76–77, 95, 109–10
trust in God, 54–62, 85–86, 112
tsunami Indian Ocean, 2004, 83
Tutu, Desmond, 17
Twells, Henry, 53

Vanhoozer, Kevin, 64
Volf, Miroslav, 17

Webster, John, 59
Wesley, John, 111

Subject and Author Index

World War I, 85

Yancey, Philip xv, 5, 42

Zedekiah, 78

www.ingramcontent.com/pod-product-compliance
Lightning Source LLC
Chambersburg PA
CBHW020854160426

43192CB00007B/927